MATHEMAT

Unit Planning
in a PLC at Work®

GRADES PREK–2

Sarah Schuhl   **Timothy D. Kanold**

Jennifer Deinhart   Nathan D. Lang-Raad

Matthew R. Larson   Nanci N. Smith

A Joint Publication With

Solution Tree | Press *a division of* Solution Tree

 NCTM® | NATIONAL COUNCIL OF TEACHERS OF MATHEMATICS

555 North Morton Street
Bloomington, IN 47404
800.733.6786 (toll free) / 812.336.7700
FAX: 812.336.7790

email: info@SolutionTree.com
SolutionTree.com

Printed in the United States of America

Library of Congress Cataloging-in-Publication Data

Names: Schuhl, Sarah, author. | Kanold, Timothy D., author. | Deinhart, Jennifer, author. | Lang, Nathan D., author. | Larson, Matthew R., author. | Smith, Nanci N., author.
Title: Mathematics unit planning in a PLC at work, grades preK-2 / Sarah Schuhl, Timothy D. Kanold, Jennifer Deinhart, Nathan D. Lang-Raad, Matthew R. Larson, Nanci N. Smith.
Description: Bloomington, IN : Solution Tree Press, [2020] | Series: Every student can learn mathematics | Includes bibliographical references and index.
Identifiers: LCCN 2020014336 (print) | LCCN 2020014337 (ebook) | ISBN 9781951075231 (paperback) | ISBN 9781951075248 (ebook)
Subjects: LCSH: Mathematics--Study and teaching (Early childhood) | Mathematics--Study and teaching (Elementary) | Curriculum planning.
Classification: LCC QA135.6 .S428 2020 (print) | LCC QA135.6 (ebook) | DDC 372.7/049--dc23
LC record available at https://lccn.loc.gov/2020014336
LC ebook record available at https://lccn.loc.gov/2020014337

Solution Tree
Jeffrey C. Jones, CEO
Edmund M. Ackerman, President

Solution Tree Press
President and Publisher: Douglas M. Rife
Associate Publisher: Sarah Payne-Mills
Art Director: Rian Anderson
Managing Production Editor: Kendra Slayton
Senior Production Editor: Suzanne Kraszewski
Content Development Specialist: Amy Rubenstein
Copy Editor: Kate St. Ives
Proofreader: Sarah Ludwig
Text and Cover Designer: Kelsey Hergül
Editorial Assistants: Sarah Ludwig and Elijah Oates

Acknowledgments

On behalf of our team of authors, Sarah Schuhl and I wish to thank all of the teachers who inspired us to write this grade-level book and mathematics unit planning series. It is through our work with you in the day-to-day reality of your classroom life that we continue to learn and grow. In addition, Jenn Deinhart deserves special kudos for her leadership of our team of authors.

We also wish to thank Solution Tree for believing in and supporting our *Every Student Can Learn Mathematics* work. Special kudos to Douglas Rife, our publisher extraordinaire, and our lead editor, Suzanne Kraszewski, who knows our work as well as we do!

Our thanks to you, too—the reader—a teacher, leader, and professional, for doing the deep work of learning together to ensure every student experiences well-planned units of mathematics study, every year.

And finally, my deep thanks to Sarah Schuhl, whose vision for this project, and her stewardship of this book, brought home the reality of our ideas with a sense of urgency and grace.

—Timothy D. Kanold

Solution Tree Press would like to thank the following reviewers:

Tracey Hulen
Mathematics Specialist
T.H. Educational Solutions
Fairfax, Virginia

Kit Norris
Author
Product Developer
Mathematics Consultant
Hudson, Massachusetts

Georgina Rivera
Elementary STEM Supervisor
Bristol Public Schools
Bristol, Connecticut

Jennifer Smith
K–4 Math Instructional Coach and Interventionist
Greenville, Wisconsin

Visit **go.SolutionTree.com/MathematicsatWork**
to download the free reproducibles in this book.

Table of Contents

About the Authors

Sarah Schuhl, MS, is an educational coach and consultant specializing in mathematics, professional learning communities (PLCs), common formative and summative assessments, school improvement, and response to intervention (RTI). She has worked in schools as a secondary mathematics teacher, high school instructional coach, and K–12 mathematics specialist.

Schuhl was instrumental in the creation of a PLC in the Centennial School District in Oregon, helping teachers make large gains in student achievement. She earned the Centennial School District Triple C Award in 2012.

Schuhl designs meaningful professional development in districts throughout the United States. Her work focuses on strengthening the teaching and learning of mathematics, having teachers learn from one another when working effectively as collaborative teams in a PLC at Work®, and striving to ensure the learning of each and every student through assessment practices and intervention. Her practical approach includes working with teachers and administrators to implement assessments for learning, analyze data, collectively respond to student learning, and map standards.

Since 2015, Schuhl has coauthored the books *Engage in the Mathematical Practices: Strategies to Build Numeracy and Literacy With K–5 Learners* and *School Improvement for All: A How-To Guide for Doing the Right Work*. She is a coauthor (with Timothy D. Kanold) of the *Every Student Can Learn Mathematics* series and the *Mathematics at Work™ Plan Book*.

Previously, Schuhl served as a member and chair of the National Council of Teachers of Mathematics (NCTM) editorial panel for the journal *Mathematics Teacher* and is currently serving as secretary of the National Council of Supervisors of Mathematics (NCSM). Her work with the Oregon Department of Education includes designing mathematics assessment items, test specifications and blueprints, and rubrics for achievement-level descriptors. She has also contributed as a writer to a middle school mathematics series and an elementary mathematics intervention program.

Schuhl earned a bachelor of science in mathematics from Eastern Oregon University and a master of science in mathematics education from Portland State University.

To learn more about Sarah Schuhl's work, follow @SSchuhl on Twitter.

Timothy D. Kanold, PhD, is an award-winning educator, author, and consultant and national thought leader in mathematics. He is former director of mathematics and science and served as superintendent of Adlai E. Stevenson High School District 125, a model PLC district in Lincolnshire, Illinois.

Dr. Kanold is committed to equity and excellence for students, faculty, and school administrators. He conducts highly motivational professional development leadership seminars worldwide with a focus on turning school vision into realized action that creates greater equity for students through the faculty and administrators' effective delivery of the PLC process.

He is a past president of the NCSM and coauthor of many best-selling mathematics textbooks over several decades. Dr. Kanold has authored or coauthored sixteen books on K–12 mathematics and school leadership since 2011, including the best-selling and IPPY 2018 Gold Medal Award–winning book *HEART!* He also has served on several writing commissions for the NCTM and has authored numerous articles and chapters on school leadership and development for education publications since 2006.

Dr. Kanold received the 2017 Ross Taylor/Glenn Gilbert Leadership Award from the NCSM, the international 2010 Damen Award for outstanding contributions to the leadership field of education from Loyola University Chicago, the 1986 Presidential Awards for Excellence in Mathematics and Science Teaching, and the 1994 Outstanding Administrator Award from the Illinois State Board of Education. He serves as an adjunct faculty member for the graduate school at Loyola University Chicago.

Dr. Kanold earned a bachelor's degree in education and a master's degree in mathematics from Illinois State University. He also completed a master's degree in educational administration at the University of Illinois and received a doctorate in educational leadership and counseling psychology from Loyola University Chicago.

To learn more about Timothy D. Kanold's work, follow @tkanold on Twitter.

Jennifer Deinhart, MEd, is an educational consultant and K–8 mathematics specialist. Deinhart is currently working as a mathematics instructional coach at Rose Hill Elementary, part of Fairfax County Public Schools. During her time at Mason Crest Elementary in Annandale, Virginia, the school was recognized as the first national model PLC school to receive the DuFour Award. A passionate educator with more than twenty years of experience working with diverse populations within Title I schools, she works collaboratively with teams of teachers to provide quality mathematics instruction.

Deinhart has been part of multiple leadership teams and now also supports schools around the nation in learning and implementing the PLC at Work process. She has worked with others to develop meaningful collaborative team structures that focus on student learning, reflecting on results, and designing instruction that meets the needs of all learners. Deinhart coauthored an article that appeared in the *Journal of Mathematics and Science: Collaborative Explorations* and has been a leader on several curriculum projects for Fairfax County Public Schools.

She received a bachelor's degree from Buffalo State College, State University of New York, and a master's of education degree specializing in K–8 mathematics leadership from George Mason University.

To learn more about Jennifer Deinhart's work, follow her at @jenn_deinhart on Twitter.

Nathan D. Lang-Raad, EdD, is a speaker, author, and consultant. He is the chief education officer at WeVideo. Throughout his career, he has served as a teacher, assistant principal, university adjunct professor, Solution Tree consultant, and partner with The Core Collaborative. He was director of elementary curriculum and instruction for Metropolitan Nashville Public Schools, as well as education supervisor at NASA's Johnson Space Center. He speaks at both local and national professional conferences and is the cofounder of Bammy Award–nominated #LeadUpChat, an educational leadership professional learning network (PLN) on Twitter. Nathan is also the cofounder of #divergED, a Twitter chat focused on divergent thinking and innovations in education. He is a Google Certified Educator, Microsoft Innovative Educator, and 2016 Apple Teacher, and he serves on the board of the Student Voice Foundation and the International Literacy Association Task Force.

Nathan is the author of *Everyday Instructional Coaching, The New Art and Science of Teaching Mathematics,* coauthored with Robert J. Marzano, and *WeVideo Every Day*. He is currently writing a book titled *The Teachers of Oz*, coauthored with Herbie Raad.

He has written several blog posts that have been featured on the EdTech K–12, Corwin Connect, Education Week, K–12 Blueprint, and the Solution Tree Blog.

Nathan received a bachelor of arts degree in general science-chemistry from Harding University in Searcy, Arkansas, a master of education degree in administration and supervision from the University of Houston-Victoria, and a doctorate of education degree in learning organizations and strategic change from David Lipscomb University in Nashville, Tennessee.

To learn more about Nathan's work, follow him on Twitter at @drlangraad.

Matthew R. Larson, PhD, is an award-winning educator and author who served as the K–12 mathematics curriculum specialist for Lincoln Public Schools in Nebraska for more than twenty years, where he currently serves as associate superintendent for instruction. He served as president of the NCTM from 2016–2018. Dr. Larson has taught mathematics at the elementary through college levels and has held an honorary appointment as a visiting associate professor of mathematics education at Teachers College, Columbia University.

He is coauthor of several mathematics textbooks, professional books, and articles on mathematics education, and was a contributing writer on the influential publications *Principles to Actions: Ensuring Mathematical Success for All* (NCTM, 2014a) and *Catalyzing Change in High School Mathematics: Initiating Critical Conversations* (NCTM, 2018). A frequent keynote speaker at national meetings, Dr. Larson's humorous presentations are well known for their application of research findings to practice.

Dr. Larson earned a bachelor's degree and doctorate from the University of Nebraska–Lincoln, where he is an adjunct professor in the department of mathematics.

To learn more about Matthew R. Larson's work, visit @mlarson_math on Twitter.

Nanci N. Smith, PhD, is currently an associate professor of mathematics and education at Arizona Christian University and part-time consultant and featured conference speaker in the areas of mathematics, curriculum and assessment, differentiated instruction, and mathematics professional learning communities. Her work includes professional development in forty-seven U.S. states and nine countries. She has taught courses at the high school, undergraduate, and graduate levels.

Nanci is author of *A Mind for Mathematics: Meaningful Teaching and Learning in Elementary Classrooms* and *Every Math Learner: A Doable Approach to Teaching With Learning Differences in Mind, Grades K–5* and *Grades 6–12*. She is coauthor of *A Handbook for Unstoppable Learning*. She is the consultant, designer, and author of the *Meaningful Mathematics: Leading Students Toward Understanding and Application* DVD series and developed a National Science Foundation–funded CD and DVD professional development series for middle school mathematics teachers. She has published various chapters in the areas of differentiation, effective mathematics instruction, curriculum design, and standards implementation and has given interviews for online publications and National Public Radio. She has been a featured speaker for the National Council of Teachers of Mathematics national conference as well as numerous other conferences in the United States and abroad.

Nanci received her PhD in curriculum and instruction, mathematics education, from Arizona State University. She is a National Board–certified teacher in Adolescence and Young Adulthood/Mathematics. Her passions are her family, especially her grandchildren, travel, and knitting. To learn more about Nanci's work, follow @DocNanci on Twitter.

To book Sarah Schuhl, Timothy D. Kanold, Jennifer Deinhart, Nathan D. Lang-Raad, Matthew R. Larson, or Nanci N. Smith for professional development, contact pd@SolutionTree.com.

Introduction

By Timothy D. Kanold

At the heart of our work as teachers of mathematics for grades preK–2 is developing student self-efficacy. *Student self-efficacy* references students' *belief* in their capability to learn the mathematics you *need students to know* by the end of each grade and as they prepare for upper elementary standards.

But what exactly *does* a preK–2 mathematics student need to know by the end of each unit of study throughout the school year? And, more important, how does a preK–2 teacher develop his or her personal self-efficacy to adequately plan for and then deliver those mathematics units of study to students?

I have been trying to answer this question throughout my entire professional life.

In 1987, I coauthored my first mathematics textbook (a geometry book for students who found mathematics a difficult subject); it was my first real experience in taking a wide body of content for the complete school year and breaking the standards down into reasonable chunks for every teacher and student to learn.

As I eventually expanded my textbook writing to include K–12 mathematics students and teachers, I realized these manageable chunks of content could vary in time length from twenty to thirty-five days, and these periods often had names like *units* or *chapters* or *modules*. I also realized just how hard it is to address a set amount of content in a specific, set time period in the early elementary grades, where the wide range of student readiness to learn mathematics provides a remarkable challenge and a need for standards to be spiraled within the curriculum throughout the early grades (meaning students work on some standards throughout the year or for longer periods of time—often to a benchmark or using daily routines).

As you know, mathematics is a vertically connected curriculum, and units of study at each grade level cannot be taught in random order; the units must exist in the right place and the right time in the mathematics story arc for each grade level, each year. There is an order to the flow of your preK–2 mathematics content story. And as preK–2 teachers, your understanding of the *how* and *why* of the content trajectories across these grades builds the foundations critical for future mathematics success in later grades.

During the work our team of mathematics authors and teachers do across the United States, we have observed elementary school mathematics programs in which focused unit planning provides your best chance of success. This book is designed to help you with the planning process for each unit of study and provide a model framework for you to use each day.

Sarah Schuhl, lead author of the unit-planning books in the *Every Student Can Learn Mathematics* series, and I realize every preK–2 mathematics teacher and teacher team needs to work collectively with their textbooks and other resources to *own* the planning process for each unit of study.

Developing *collective teacher efficacy* is at the heart of the Professional Learning Community (PLC) at Work® process. Sabina Rak Neugebauer, Megan Hopkins, and

James P. Spillane (2019) highlight the importance of a collective approach anchored in content with the words, "Social interactions firmly anchored in instructional practice can move teachers beyond contrived collegiality to a culture that can in turn influence a teacher's sense of efficacy" (p. 13). Teachers have discussions of mathematics content they are teaching each week and then place those episodes into manageable chunks of content for their team's discussion and work.

In 2019, when Solution Tree asked Sarah Schuhl and me to develop the *Mathematics at Work™ Plan Book* (Kanold & Schuhl, 2020), we jumped at the chance to provide a book that would help you organize your mathematics work and story arc for the entire school year. The weekly planners we created for the book provide helpful organizational tools and may be completely sufficient for your team. However, we also realize you might need more specific direction with the elements of planning we ask you to prepare for each unit of mathematics study.

The coauthors of this Mathematics at Work unit-planning guide for grades preK–2 (Sarah Schuhl, Jennifer Deinhart, Nathan Lang-Raad, Nanci Smith, Matt Larson, and I) serve or have served in many mathematics teaching and leading roles. One such role is to serve on our Mathematics at Work team of national thought leaders. As we travel around the United States helping elementary school teachers improve student learning in mathematics, preK–2 educators often ask us, "How do you collectively plan for a unit of study in mathematics at our grade level?"

The answer to that question is the hope and promise of this book.

The Purpose of This Book

We want to help your grade-level team learn *how to* work together to perform the following seven collaborative tasks for each unit of mathematics study throughout the year.

Generate Essential Learning Standards for Each Unit

Unwrap standards into daily learning targets, and write those standards in student-friendly language for essential learning standards. And then use those essential learning standards to drive feedback on common

mathematics assessments, classwork, independent practice, and intervention as a collaborative team.

Create a Team Unit Calendar

Decide the number of days needed to teach each essential learning standard and the start and end dates for the unit. Determine the dates to administer any common mid-unit or end-of-unit assessments or the dates you might use to administer any ongoing assessments to individual or small groups of students. Establish each date the team will analyze data from any common mid-unit and end-of-unit assessments to plan a team response to student learning.

Identify Prior Knowledge

Determine and identify the recent prerequisite content knowledge students need to access the grade-level learning in each unit of study. Decide which mathematical activities (tasks or prompts) to use for students to connect the prior knowledge at the start of each lesson throughout the unit. Use these activities to discern student readiness and entry points into each lesson.

Determine Vocabulary and Notations

Identify the academic vocabulary students will be hearing, reading, and using during discourse throughout the unit. Identify any mathematical notations students will need to read, write, and speak during the unit.

Identify Resources and Activities

Determine which lessons in the team's current basal curriculum materials align to the essential learning standards in the unit. Determine examples of higher- and lower-level tasks (including games) students must engage in to fully learn each essential learning standard.

Agree on Tools and Technology

PreK–2 teachers use many tools to teach mathematics to students. Determine any manipulatives or sources of technology needed to help students master the essential learning standards of the unit. Identify whether the tools or technology needed for the unit will support student learning of the essential learning standards with a focus on conceptual understanding, application, or procedural fluency. Identify which tools and technology, if any, will be part of instruction or common assessments.

Record Reflection and Notes

When planning the unit, record notes of things to remember when teaching (by answering, for example, these questions: What are the expectations for quality student work, written or observed? Which mathematical strategies should teachers use throughout each unit for learning?). After the unit, reflect on instruction and assessment changes to the unit, and record ideas to use when planning the unit for next year.

The Parts of This Book

Part 1 provides detailed insight into how your mathematics team can effectively respond to these seven planning tasks for the essential standards you expect students to learn in grades preK–2.

Part 2 provides four detailed model mathematics units related to foundations of addition and subtraction (one for each grade level) and describes a number reasoning story arc for preK–2 related to joining and separating and addition and subtraction number operations. We hope part 2 provides an inspiring model for your grade-level team.

The epilogue shares an example for how to organize your elementary grade-level team's work on a unit-by-unit basis so you can grow and learn from its work in future years. If your collaborative team does not already have a mathematics unit of study yearlong plan with standards, appendix A (page 137) provides a proficiency map protocol as a way to organize your standards and to determine when students should be proficient with each standard. Finally, appendix B (page 139) contains a team checklist and questions for your team to answer as you plan each mathematics unit. Appendix B summarizes the elements of unit planning shared in parts 1 and 2 of this book and is intended to be a quick reference to guide the work of your team in your unit planning.

A Final Thought

You might wonder, "Why is this book titled *Mathematics Unit Planning in a PLC at Work, Grades PreK–2*?" In 1980, my second mathematics teaching job landed me on the doorstep of an educational leader who would later start an education movement in the United States that would spread throughout North America and even worldwide. He was the architect of the Professional Learning Communities at Work movement (along with Robert Eaker) and my principal for many years. Richard DuFour expected every grade-level or course-based team in our school district to answer four critical questions for each unit of study in mathematics (DuFour, DuFour, Eaker, Many, & Mattos, 2016).

1. What do we want all students to know and be able to do? (essential learning standards)

2. How will we know if they know it? (lesson-design elements, assessments, and tasks used)

3. How will we respond if they don't know it? (formative assessment processes)

4. How will we respond if they do know it? (formative assessment processes)

As your collaborative team pursues the deep work, remember it all begins with a robust and well-planned response to PLC critical question 1 (*What do we want all students to know and be able to do?*). That is the focus of our grades preK–2 unit planning book.

We want to help you plan for and answer the first question for each mathematics unit, grade level, and student. We wish you the best in your mathematics teaching and learning journey, *together*.

PART 1

Mathematics Unit Planning
and Design Elements

*Creating a guaranteed, viable
curriculum is the number-one factor
for increased levels of learning.*

—Robert J. Marzano

PART 1

As your prekindergarten, kindergarten, first-, or second-grade team clarifies what students will learn in mathematics at each grade level, it brings a laser-like focus to the content and processes students must learn in each unit throughout the year. Your team clarifies the depth of learning required for students to become proficient with the mathematics standards, and you and your team members build a shared understanding of the content students must learn in each unit of study. *Together*, you determine the mathematics your team must teach and assess throughout each unit.

The action of intentional planning as a team for student learning of mathematics on a unit-by-unit basis develops your individual and team collective teacher efficacy.

Working together with your colleagues as a collaborative mathematics team, you erase the inequities in student learning expectations that otherwise could exist across a grade level or course. Together, you and your team determine what students must know and be able to do. Then, your team does the work to ensure every student learns through the agreed-on, high-quality instruction, common assessments, and formative assessment processes. Your team recognizes the many challenges inherent to students learning robust mathematics standards and takes collective responsibility to close gaps and extend learning as needed.

To erase inequities and ensure grade-level learning of mathematics for each student, your primary-level team begins with an agreed-on guaranteed and viable curriculum for mathematics. Your team works to ensure students learn identified essential mathematics standards within the school year.

On a unit-by-unit basis, your team builds a shared understanding of the essential mathematics standards students must learn. PLC experts and coauthors Richard DuFour, Rebecca DuFour, Robert Eaker, Thomas W. Many, and Mike Mattos (2016) explain that your shared understanding will:

- Promote clarity among your colleagues about what students must learn

- Ensure consistent curricular priorities among colleagues

- Help develop the common pacing required for effective common assessments

- Ensure the curriculum is *viable* (that you can teach in the allotted time)

- Create ownership among all teachers required to teach the intended curriculum

It might be surprising, but in a PLC at Work, teacher teams build mathematics units from the standards, not from the chapters in a textbook. Too often, textbooks include more learning than your state or province may require, or the textbooks may be missing content that you need to supplement to better match the standards and local curriculum expectations. Thus, your team starts with making sense of the standards students must learn in each unit of study, and then utilizes the most effective resources for teaching and learning.

Part 1 consists of two chapters. Chapter 1 (page 9) describes the mathematics content and skills students must learn in grades preK–2. Your team's work begins by understanding *what* mathematics students must learn in each of the primary grades, preK, K, 1, and 2. Chapter 2 (page 15) provides protocols and tools your grade-level collaborative team can use to plan for the student learning each mathematics unit requires. Together, your team's understanding of the mathematics content students must learn and your framework for units allows for a backward-design approach to ensuring every student learns mathematics.

CHAPTER 1

Planning for Student Learning of Mathematics in Grades PreK–2

*Mathematics is a conceptual domain. It is not, as many people think,
a list of facts and methods to be remembered.*

—Jo Boaler

The first critical question of a PLC is, What do we expect all students to know and be able to do? (DuFour et al., 2016). As your collaborative team successfully answers this question for each unit of study, members build a common understanding of the mathematics students learn in your grade level. What is the mathematics story that unfolds as student learning progresses from one mathematics unit to the next? How do the units fit together and build on one another within and across the primary grades from preK to second grade?

Guaranteed and Viable Curriculum

Your preK, kindergarten, first-, or second-grade team effectively backward plans the year by grouping essential mathematics standards into units to create the guaranteed and viable mathematics curriculum students must learn. The order in which you teach the mathematics units provides the framework for your grade-level mathematics story. Within each unit, your daily lessons create the beginning, middle, and end for that part of the story.

Thus, evidence of your team's guaranteed and viable curriculum includes (1) a yearlong pacing plan of standards and benchmarks throughout the year of spiraled standards (proficiency map or pacing guide), (2) unit plans, and (3) daily lessons. The graphic in figure 1.1 illustrates these three areas of team planning for a mathematics guaranteed and viable curriculum.

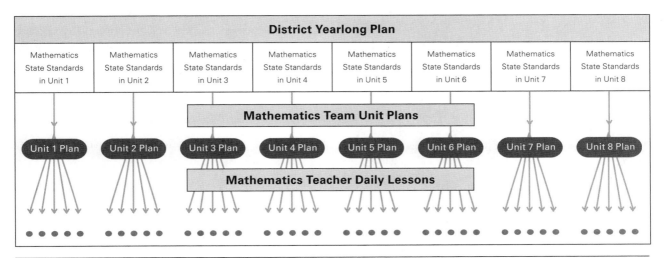

Figure 1.1: Mathematics guaranteed and viable curriculum plan.

Together, the mathematics units of study tell the story of the primary grade-level standards teachers expect students to learn throughout the year and from one year to the next.

As figure 1.1 (page 9) shows, your grade-level team's guaranteed and viable curriculum is first defined by a district yearlong pacing guide or proficiency map (showing a time line for student proficiency with each mathematics standard). Your team then determines a time frame appropriate to each mathematics unit, typically two to four weeks in duration in the primary grades. This process eliminates the potential risk of running out of time and skipping units or essential standards that fall at the end of the year.

If your collaborative team does not have a year-long plan with standards in clearly defined units, see appendix A (page 137), "Create a Proficiency Map," for additional support. Helping each teacher on your team become comfortable with the progression of mathematics units throughout the school year will support your students' understanding of the mathematics story arc for various standards.

Mathematics Unit Planner

Once your team determines the mathematics units for your grade level (detailing the standards and time line for each unit) for the year, your collaborative team can plan for student learning on a *unit-by-unit* basis (see figure 1.2; Kanold & Schuhl, 2020).

The Mathematics Unit Planner in figure 1.2 provides a template your team can use as you develop a shared understanding of what students are expected to learn in each unit of study. The numbered sections in the Mathematics Unit Planner correspond with the seven elements of unit planning. Throughout this book, you will see numbered headings that correspond with these seven areas. (Find completed examples of unit planners for preK in figure 3.12 [page 58], kindergarten in figure 4.11 [page 79], first grade in figure 5.11 [page 105], and second grade in figure 6.11 [page 129].)

Once the elements of the Mathematics Unit Planner (see figure 1.2) are complete, your team can use the information to plan for common assessments and daily lesson design (see *Mathematics Assessment and Intervention in a PLC at Work* [Kanold, Schuhl, et al., 2018] and *Mathematics Instruction and Tasks in a PLC at Work* [Kanold, Kanold-McIntyre, et al., 2018]).

Additionally, you and your collaborative team can reference the unit planner for each successive unit in the year and from one year to the next as your team continues to deepen its own understanding of the required student learning.

In *Principles to Actions*, the National Council of Teachers of Mathematics (NCTM, 2014a) shares, "Effective mathematics teaching begins with a shared understanding among teachers of the mathematics that students are learning and how this mathematics develops along learning progressions" (p. 12). Therefore, before diving into each individual unit plan for the year, as a team, first consider the mathematical content students are learning in your grade. Additionally, make sense of the mathematical content trajectories, or progressions, that students are learning across your preK–2 band.

Mathematics Concepts and Skills for Grades PreK–2

Students in grades preK–2 develop their understanding of number, place value, and addition and subtraction. They grow their knowledge related to geometry and measurement. Throughout these foundational primary years, students first learn to count sequentially and read, write, and name numbers. They determine how to quantify a group of objects using a number. They compare numbers and learn to conceptualize the differences in value represented by two or more numbers. They also develop flexibility with numbers and use patterns to grow place-value understanding. In geometry, students identify, describe, compose, decompose, and analyze two- and three-dimensional shapes and, by second grade, create arrays for early multiplication understanding. They partition circles and rectangles to begin building an understanding of fractions. Through measurement and data, students develop an understanding of linear measurements, time, and money.

Table 1.1 (page 12) shows some of the key mathematics concepts teachers expect students to learn in grades preK–2. Timing for teaching these key concepts is driven by grade and by the vertical trajectory NCTM's (2006) *Curriculum Focal Points for Prekindergarten Through Grade 8 Mathematics* first defines. These key mathematical concepts give an overview of the more specific local standards your team will teach each unit.

Unit: _____

Start Date: _____   End Date: _____   Total Number of Days: _____

Unit Planning

❶ Essential Learning Standards

List the essential learning standards for this unit.

❸ Prior Knowledge

List standards from a previous unit or grade students will access in this unit.

❹ Vocabulary and Notations

List the mathematical academic vocabulary and notations for this unit.

❺ Possible Resources or Activities

List the possible resources or activities to use when teaching the essential learning standards.

❻ Tools and Technology

List the essential tools, manipulatives, and technology needed for this unit.

❼ Reflection and Notes

After the unit, reflect and list what to do again, revise, or change.

❷ Unit Calendar

	Monday	Tuesday	Wednesday	Thursday	Friday
Week 1					
Week 2					
Week 3					
Week 4					
Week 5					

Source: Adapted from Kanold & Schuhl, 2020, p. 30.

Figure 1.2: Mathematics Unit Planner.

*Visit **go.SolutionTree.com/MathematicsatWork** for a free reproducible version of this figure.*

Table 1.1: Mathematics Concepts and Skills for Grades PreK–2

	PreK	Kindergarten	Grade 1	Grade 2
Counting and Cardinality	• Develop an understanding of whole numbers, including concepts of correspondence to 10, counting verbally to 10, and cardinality. • Identify numerals 0–10. • Compare groups of objects to 10.	• Represent and develop an understanding of whole numbers, including concepts of correspondence to 20, counting to 100, and comparing groups of objects. • Write numbers to 20 and compare numerals to 10.	• Count and write numbers to 120.	• Count, read, and write numbers to 1,000. • Skip count by 2s, 5s, 10s, and 100s.
Operations and Algebraic Thinking	• Explore addition and subtraction using practical real-life situations, objects, pictures, sounds, and so on. • Compose numbers to 5 or 10.	• Represent addition and subtraction with objects, pictures, sounds, expressions, and equations to 10. • Fluently add and subtract within 5.	• Develop understanding of addition, subtraction, and strategies for addition and subtraction within 20. • Fluently add and subtract within 10.	• Develop fluency with addition, subtraction, and strategies for addition and subtraction within 100. • Fluently add and subtract within 20.
Number and Operations in Base Ten	• Investigate the relationship between a set of objects and a group (for example, group of 2 objects, 5 objects, 10 objects, and so on).	• Compose and decompose numbers from 11–19 using a ten and ones.	• Develop understanding of whole-number relationships and place value, including grouping in tens and ones. • Compare two two-digit numbers. • Add special cases within 100 using models, pictures, and strategies.	• Extend place-value understanding to three-digit numbers, including groupings of hundreds, tens, and ones. • Compare two three-digit numbers. • Develop fluency with multidigit addition and subtraction.
Measurement and Data	• Identify measurable attributes of objects. • Compare objects using measurable attributes.	• Sort and order objects by measurable attributes.	• Develop understanding of linear measurement and measuring lengths as iterating length units. • Tell and write time in hours and half hours. • Organize, represent, and interpret data with up to three categories.	• Develop an understanding of linear measurement and facility in measuring lengths. • Tell and write time to the nearest five minutes. • Solve word problems involving money. • Create and solve problems using a picture or bar graph.
Geometry	• Identify and describe two-dimensional shapes (circles, triangles, rectangles, including squares that are special rectangles). • Describe three-dimensional shapes and sort them.	• Identify and describe two- and three-dimensional shapes. • Compose simple shapes to form larger shapes.	• Build and draw shapes with given attributes. • Compose and decompose two- or three-dimensional shapes. • Partition circles and rectangles into two and four equal shares.	• Identify and draw shapes with given attributes. • Partition a rectangle into an array. • Partition circles and rectangles into two, three, or four equal shares.

Source: Adapted from NCTM, 2006.

In grades preK–2, students are developing an understanding of number and number relationships to develop number sense and mathematical reasoning. In preK and kindergarten, students learn how to count and use numbers to determine how many objects are in a set and to subitize (tell how many objects they see without counting; for example, roll a die and see five without counting all five dots). Students learn that each number means one more in terms of quantity, and they compare numbers using groups of objects, and later, numerals. Students write numbers to 20 by the end of kindergarten, 120 in first grade, and 1,000 in second grade.

Operations and algebraic thinking in preK–2 focuses on students making connections between counting and the operations of addition and subtraction. Students use strategies to make sense of and solve addition and subtraction word problems within a given set of numbers. Students are expected to find the missing value in different parts of the equation. Students use models, drawings, and equations to represent their thinking. Within this strand, students also develop fluency with addition and subtraction within 5 by kindergarten, 10 in first grade, and 20 in second grade. Your team should keep in mind that NCTM (2014b) defines *fluency* as students having efficient, accurate, and flexible procedures, not as the ability to complete a given number of problems in a specified number of seconds or minutes.

Students develop *number sense* by thinking flexibly with numbers and understanding the relationships between numbers and operations. They develop an understanding of magnitude of number and how the number system works beginning in preK. Students start with ones in preK and end with hundreds, tens, and ones in second grade with an additional understanding of 1,000. Place value provides a way to compare numbers, make sense of addition and subtraction strategies using tools and drawings, and apply properties of operations related to addition and subtraction with larger numbers. Using base-ten place value, students can add 13 + 24 by adding 1 ten + 2 tens to get 3 tens and 3 ones + 4 ones to get 7 ones, for a total of 3 tens 7 ones which is 37.

For *measurement and data*, students learn to recognize measurable attributes and apply that learning to compare objects. Students in first grade begin to measure length indirectly and strengthen their sense of numbers while counting and comparing units of length. This learning extends to second grade where students use standard units and measuring tools. Students in first and second grade also begin to display data in bar and picture graphs and answer questions about those graphs. In first grade, students tell and write time to the nearest half hour and to the nearest five minutes in second grade. Students in second grade also solve word problems related to money. Teachers in preK–1 can introduce students to money as they discuss base-ten numbers, using dimes for tens, pennies for ones, and dollars for hundreds.

In the area of *geometry*, students identify and name two- and three-dimensional shapes. Students also compose shapes, making a connection to how they also compose numbers. In preK and kindergarten, students identify shapes in the world and begin to sort shapes. In first and second grade, students begin to partition circles and rectangles as an introduction to fractions in third grade. In second grade, students build an array as an introduction to multiplication understanding in third grade.

Your team may want to explore mathematics learning progressions as defined in your state standards or reference online mathematics learning progression documents, such as those developed by the Common Core Standards Writing Team (n.d.) or Achieve the Core's (n.d.) coherence map. Your team may also want to engage in a book study, perhaps referencing NCTM resources related to understanding the essential content and skills needed for mathematics in preK–2, such as *Catalyzing Change in Early Childhood and Elementary Mathematics: Initiating Critical Conversations* (NCTM, 2020). You might also consider *Mathematics Learning in Early Childhood: Paths Toward Excellence and Equity* (Cross, Woods, & Schweingruber, 2009). This resource provides great insight into mathematics teaching and learning at the early childhood level, including preK.

With so much mathematics content to learn, your team's planning of units helps your team to ensure a guaranteed and viable mathematics curriculum within your grade level and across grades preK–2. Planning the units together to more deeply learn your own grade-level content and its importance in the primary grade trajectory builds teacher team self-efficacy.

Connections Between Mathematics Content and Unit Planning

For each mathematics unit in your grade level, you support your team's progress toward better understanding of the standards that support the guaranteed and viable mathematics curriculum. Together, you and your team use the Mathematics Unit Planner in figure 1.2 (page 11) to record answers to the following questions.

- What exactly do students need to know and be able to do in this unit?

- Which mathematics standards should we commonly assess? When?

- How does the mathematics learning in this unit connect to the standards students must learn in previous or future units?

- Which academic mathematics vocabulary and notations must students learn to read, write, and speak in the unit to be proficient with the standards?

- What are examples of higher- and lower-level-cognitive-demand mathematical tasks students should be able to demonstrate proficiency with if they have learned the standards?

- Which mathematical tools or technology should students learn or utilize to demonstrate an understanding of the standards in the unit?

Answering these questions as a team creates more equitable student learning experiences from one teacher to the next. Additionally, developing your teacher efficacy strengthens your instructional practices. Consequently, student learning improves because your entire team is working to ensure each student *learns* the organized mathematics content from one unit to the next.

Chapter 2 provides tools and protocols that help your preK, kindergarten, first-, or second-grade mathematics team unpack standards in the unit and learn how to intentionally address each unit-planning element as you develop your mathematics story arc for the school year.

Unit Planning as a Collaborative Mathematics Team

Teams must develop units of instruction that support the pacing guide and know specifically when they will teach and assess each of the essential standards or learning targets.

—Kim Bailey and Chris Jakicic

As a collaborative team in a PLC at Work, you seek to answer the following four critical questions.

1. What do we expect all students to know and be able to do?

2. How will we know if students learn it?

3. How will we respond when some students do not learn?

4. How will we extend the learning for students who are already proficient? (DuFour et al., 2016)

To fully address these questions as a collaborative mathematics team, members perform several tasks together (Kanold, Barnes, et al., 2018; Kanold, Kanold-McIntyre, et al., 2018; Kanold, Schuhl, et al., 2018; Kanold, Toncheff, et al., 2018) such as the following.

- Make sense of essential standards.

- Create common mid-unit and end-of-unit assessments with scoring agreements.

- Analyze common assessment data.

- Design high-quality, research-affirmed lessons.

- Create independent practice assignments.

- Give consistent feedback to students.

- Involve students in their own learning.

Mathematics Unit Planning as a Team

The self-reflection protocol in figure 2.1 (page 16) is a tool you can use to ask each member of your collaborative team about his or her current mathematics unit planning practices. The team can then use each member's responses to find some initial common ground. Share your individual responses as a collaborative team to examine variances in individual teacher practices and build team consensus.

In his book *In Praise of American Educators*, Richard DuFour (2015) states:

> Collaborative teams of teachers responsible for teaching the same subject or grade level should be engaged in a collaborative process to:
>
> - Study the intended standards together
> - Agree on priorities within the standards
> - Clarify how the standards translate into student knowledge, skills, and dispositions
> - Establish what proficient work looks like
> - Develop general pacing guidelines for delivering the curriculum
> - Most importantly, commit to one another that they will, in fact, teach the agreed-on curriculum, unit by unit (pp. 145–146)

As your team engages in the type of collaborative unit planning DuFour (2015) describes, use the Mathematics Unit Planning Rubric in figure 2.2 (page 17) as a tool to rate and evaluate your mathematics unit planning practices for each unit. How does your team score? Does it score a 12, 15, or 20? How close do you score to 28 out of a possible 28?

You should expect to eventually score 4s on all seven elements of the Mathematics Unit Planning Rubric (see

Mathematics Team Discussion Tool for Unit Planning

Directions: Use the following prompts to guide discussion about your unit planning practices.

For questions 1–6: When planning mathematics units . . .

1. How do you identify and make sense of the specific mathematics state standards students must learn?

2. How do you determine calendar dates for the beginning and end of the unit, as well as for any common assessments?

3. How do you identify the prior knowledge students have already learned that connects to the current unit?

4. How do you determine the academic vocabulary and notations students will learn during the unit?

5. How do you identify resources and activities to ensure the balanced use of higher- and lower-level-cognitive-demand mathematical tasks?

6. How do you decide on the tools and technology to use to strengthen student learning?

7. When a unit ends, how does your team reflect on the strengths and weaknesses of the unit and electronically document what to keep or change for the same mathematics unit next year?

Figure 2.1: Mathematics team discussion tool for unit planning.

*Visit **go.SolutionTree.com/MathematicsatWork** for a free reproducible version of this figure.*

High-Quality Unit-Planning Elements	Description of Level 1	Requirements of the Indicator Are Not Present	Limited Requirements of the Indicator Are Present	Substantially Meets the Requirements of the Indicator	Fully Achieves the Requirements of the Indicator	Description of Level 4 (A rating of 4 means the team completes the indicator together before the unit begins.)
1. Generate essential learning standards.	Teachers do not discuss or agree on the standards students will learn, nor do they create uniform essential learning standards for the unit.	1	2	3	4	The team makes sense of the standards students must learn in the unit and generates essential learning standards all students routinely use throughout the unit.
2. Create a team unit calendar.	Teachers agree on the next unit to teach, but do not determine common pacing of essential learning standards or the dates and use of common assessments.	1	2	3	4	The team determines critical dates for the unit that include the start and end of the unit, common assessments, the analysis of data, flex days needed, and the daily progression of learning in lessons.
3. Identify prior knowledge.	Each teacher independently determines the prior knowledge students need to have learned to access learning in the current unit.	1	2	3	4	The team determines the prior-knowledge standards students need to know to make connections to new learning, and discusses how to engage students in reviewing that prior knowledge.
4. Determine vocabulary and notations.	Each teacher independently determines the academic vocabulary and notations to emphasize throughout the unit.	1	2	3	4	The team determines the academic vocabulary and notations to teach and assess throughout the unit, and discusses how to engage students in using both for clear mathematics communication.
5. Identify resources and activities.	Each teacher independently selects the lessons to teach and the tasks to use for learning. Lessons and tasks may not match the essential learning standards or reflect a rigor balance of higher- and lower-level reasoning.	1	2	3	4	The team identifies curriculum resources to use for teaching mathematics that match the essential learning standards. They determine examples of higher- and lower-level mathematical tasks in which students need to become proficient for each essential learning standard.
6. Agree on tools and technology.	Each teacher independently determines the tools and technology students will use during lessons and assessments.	1	2	3	4	The team agrees on the most effective tools and technology all students will use to learn concepts and which ones students can select from when taking common assessments.
7. Record reflection and notes.	Each teacher (without a team discussion) plans elements of the unit plan. At the end of the unit, the team does not record a reflection on what to keep or change for the next school year.	1	2	3	4	When planning a unit, the team records any notes to remember for instruction and assessments once the unit begins. At the end of the unit, the team reflects on the strengths and weaknesses of the unit and records what to keep or change for next year.

Figure 2.2: Mathematics Unit Planning Rubric.

Visit go.SolutionTree.com/MathematicsatWork for a free reproducible version of this figure.

figure 2.2, page 17). Determine your team's strengths and weaknesses related to unit planning using the rubric. Challenge yourself and your team members to grow toward the level 4 descriptors for each element of unit planning. (Also note that the seven elements of unit planning appear in the order your team should address each action, and note that the numbers on the rubric and in the unit planner correspond with the sections throughout this book to guide your work as a team.)

Any collaborative team plan for a mathematics unit first requires a shared understanding of the essential learning standards students must learn in that unit. The Mathematics Unit Planning Rubric in figure 2.2 (page 17) and the Mathematics Unit Planner in figure 1.2 (page 11) begin with identifying the essential learning standards.

❶ Essential Learning Standards

Essential learning standards are the critical skills, knowledge, and dispositions each student must acquire as a result of each course, grade level, and unit of instruction—"the deep understandings that are important for students to remember long after they have forgotten how to carry out specific techniques or apply particular formulas" (NCTM, 2018, p. 17). Essential learning standards are the big ideas of each unit, written as *I can . . .* statements, and may also be referenced as *power standards*, *priority standards*, or *promise standards* (Kanold & Schuhl, 2020).

Your team's guaranteed and viable curriculum should have between three to six essential learning standards in each unit. These three to six clustered mathematics standards act as the driver for the following.

- Determining the *why* of your mathematics lessons

- Organizing the questions on your common mathematics unit quizzes and tests

- Providing a targeted way for your team to analyze student learning

- Implementing student intervention and support during and after a unit of study

- Deciding the prerequisite skills to address or extensions to implement based on the learning focus of the unit

- Establishing how students will name what they have learned (or not learned yet) when reflecting on their assessment results or learning activities

Establishing the essential learning standards as a team for each mathematics unit is critical to student learning through quality unit instruction and assessment. Together, your team members will determine what every student needs to learn so you can work together to ensure that learning.

Your yearlong pacing guide or proficiency map (see figure 1.1, page 9) should account for the preK, kindergarten, first-, and second-grade mathematics standards students should learn in a year (see appendix A, page 137). However, your team may have more standards than students can learn well in a given school year. Educators and researchers such as Douglas B. Reeves (2002); Larry Ainsworth (2003); Grant Wiggins and Jay McTighe (2011); Richard DuFour et al. (2016); Austin Buffum, Mike Mattos, and Janet Malone (2018); and Timothy D. Kanold, Sarah Schuhl, et al. (2018) write about the need to rank your mathematics standards in order of importance and focus on those that are deemed most essential. Your team may want to consult resources from NCTM or Achieve the Core (www.achievethecore.org) to help prioritize the importance of your state standards.

Figure 2.3 shows one possible way to sort standards by putting them in *need-to-know*, *important-to-know*, and *nice-to-know* categories. Your team uses need-to-know and important-to-know standards in the unit to generate the essential learning standards for each unit. The need-to-know standards drive your common mid-unit assessments and Tier 2 interventions. These are the standards your team agrees must first inform team interventions when students have not yet learned them.

Together, your team will unwrap the essential state standards (both the need-to-know and important-to-know standards) in the unit. The unwrapping process will clarify "the broader mathematical goals that guide planning on a unit-by-unit basis, as well as the more targeted mathematics goals that guide instructional decisions on a lesson-by-lesson basis" (NCTM, 2014a, p. 12).

Figure 2.4 (page 20) is a team protocol to use when generating essential learning standards for a unit and building a shared understanding of what students must

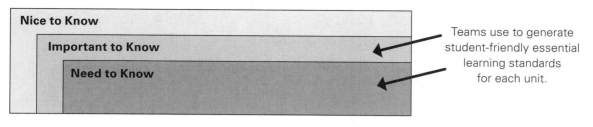

Figure 2.3: Importance-sorting system for mathematics standards.

know and be able to do for each standard. The protocol includes creating one or two student-friendly *I can* statements for each essential learning standard for student reflection and assessment. Your team also determines vocabulary, student proficiency levels, and examples of tasks to match the intent of the standard. Additionally, through the unwrapping process, this protocol helps your team create daily learning targets for lessons and address other critical elements of strong unit planning practices. Grade-level mathematics standard examples appear in figures 3.1–3.4 (pages 41–45), 4.1–4.3 (pages 64–66), 5.1–5.3 (pages 86–90), and 6.1–6.3 (pages 111–115) for units in grades preK–2 related to *counting and cardinality, addition and subtraction to 10, addition and subtraction to 20,* and *multidigit addition and subtraction.*

The three to six essential learning standards in each unit determine how to cluster the unit content for assessment and grading purposes, as well as for student reflection and intervention. However, the essential learning standards do not clarify daily learning targets used in each lesson needed to reflect the conceptual understanding, procedural fluency, or applications a student must demonstrate to show his or her understanding of each essential learning standard (Kanold, Kanold-McIntyre, et al., 2018).

Your team will need to consider the *story of learning* in the unit through the lens of daily learning targets. Address such questions as, "Why should each lesson be taught?" "Why should one lesson follow another?" and "Which tasks are needed for students to demonstrate proficiency each day?" PreK, kindergarten, first-, and second-grade teams work together to determine how the daily learning targets grow a student's learning of each essential learning standard, and to determine the *why* of each lesson. For more information related to designing high-quality lessons, see *Mathematics Instruction and Tasks in a PLC at Work* (Kanold,

Kanold-McIntyre, et al., 2018). (Visit **go.SolutionTree .com/MathematicsatWork** for free reproducibles.)

When your team unwraps each standard for the unit, it generates the daily learning targets. The conceptual understanding and procedural knowledge and skills in figure 2.4 (page 20) list what students must know and be able to do—the daily learning targets. Your team determines the order to address each standard, and then creates a storyboard of learning for students within the mathematics unit.

Figure 2.5 (page 22) illustrates *how* the state standards, essential learning standards for assessment and student reflection, and daily learning targets fit together. Because the information impacts your team's common assessments and instruction, figure 2.5 (page 22) also appears in *Mathematics Assessment and Intervention in a PLC at Work* (Kanold, Schuhl, et al., 2018) and *Mathematics Instruction and Tasks in a PLC at Work* (Kanold, Kanold-McIntyre, et al., 2018). (Visit **go.SolutionTree.com/MathematicsatWork** for free reproducibles.) Examples for grades preK–2 foundations of addition and subtraction units appear in figures 3.5 (page 47), 4.4 (page 68), 5.4 (page 91), and 6.4 (page 117) in part 2 of this book.

Once your collaborative team clarifies the essential learning standards and daily learning targets for a unit, you are ready to determine a mathematics unit calendar.

❷ Unit Calendar

Pacing the unit on a calendar allows your team to make critical decisions about how to emphasize time for student learning and assessment of essential mathematics learning standards. When should the unit begin? When should the unit end? When will your team provide common assessments during the unit? Place the general dates into a calendar to provide

Directions: Identify mathematics state standards students will be learning in a unit. Complete the protocol for each mathematics standard to build a shared team understanding of what students must know and be able to do for each.

Complete the template on page 21 using the following directions to make sense of each team mathematics standard and generate the information needed to more intentionally plan for student learning in the unit.

1. Write the mathematics state standard.

2. Circle the verbs in the state standard that identify student actions, and underline the content in noun phrases.

3. List the underlined phrases and add any clarification as needed in the following table under the heading Conceptual Understanding: What Do Students Need to Know?

4. Pair verbs with the content list in the table under the heading Procedural Knowledge and Skills: What Do Students Need to Do? Both of these lists become daily learning targets to consider when designing lessons and assessing student knowledge.

5. Identify any academic mathematics vocabulary and notations students will need in order to read, write, and become proficient with each standard.

6. Generate student-friendly essential learning standards (*I can* statements) for student assessment analysis and reflection.

7. Determine what a student must do to be proficient with the standard, as well as how a student might show a minimal, partial, or advanced understanding of the standard.

8. Determine exemplar mathematics tasks that show the complexity of reasoning required when students demonstrate proficiency with the essential mathematics standard.

Unit:

State Standard in the Unit:

Conceptual Understanding: What Do Students Need to Know?	Procedural Knowledge and Skills: What Do Students Need to Do?

Academic Vocabulary and Notations

Essential Learning Standards (in Student-Friendly Language—I can . . .)

Proficiency Level of Understanding	
4 Advanced	
3 Proficient	
2 Partial	
1 Minimal	

Exemplar Tasks to Meet Standard:

Source: Adapted from Kramer & Schuhl, 2017.

Figure 2.4: Team protocol to unwrap and make sense of mathematics standards.

*Visit **go.SolutionTree.com/MathematicsatWork** for a free reproducible version of this figure.*

Directions: (1) Write the unit state standards in the left column. If two or more parts of standards or full standards align to the same student-friendly essential learning standard, group them together in that same cell. (2) Write the essential learning standards for the unit in the center column using student-friendly language. (3) List the possible progression of daily learning targets for each essential standard using the lists your team generated for conceptual understanding and procedural knowledge and skills in the team protocol to unwrap and make sense of mathematics standards (see figure 2.4, page 20).

Unit: _____

Formal Unit Standards (State Standard Language)	Essential Learning Standards for Assessment and Reflection (Student-Friendly Language)	Daily Learning Targets What students must know and be able to do for each lesson (unwrapped standards) (Storyboard Progression)
	I can . . .	
	I can . . .	
	I can . . .	
	I can . . .	
	I can . . .	

Source: Adapted from Kanold, Kanold-McIntyre, et al., 2018; Kanold, Schuhl, et al., 2018.

Figure 2.5: Mathematics unit standards, essential learning standards, and daily learning targets.

Visit go.SolutionTree.com/MathematicsatWork for a free reproducible version of this figure.

progress guidelines for your team's planning for the required number of lessons, assessments, and assignment days for the unit.

As *Mathematics Assessment and Intervention in a PLC at Work* (Kanold, Schuhl, et al., 2018) notes, your team must also schedule time for students to reflect on their learning and plan team-designed Tier 2 interventions as needed. (Visit **go.SolutionTree .com/MathematicsatWork** for free reproducibles.) Interventions and extensions should take place during a designated intervention time during your school day or through the use of a *flex day*—a day in the unit when each teacher on your team can re-engage students in learning as needed. Consider how your team will create time for a meaningful instructional response to learning based on the common assessment dates on the calendar.

Author and assessment consultant Nicole Dimich (2015) states, "A common assessment calendar can help a team organize how to best use common formative assessments to inform learning" (p. 109). The protocol in figure 2.6 (page 24) shares the team agreements necessary when planning each unit using a calendar (see the *Mathematics at Work Plan Book* [Kanold & Schuhl, 2020]). Completed grade-level examples for foundations of addition and subtraction units appear in figures 3.6 (page 48), 4.5 (page 69), 5.5 (page 93), and 6.5 (page 118).

Keep in mind, in the primary grades, your team may give ongoing assessments (one-on-one brief assessments given over the course of a day or several days). Your team calendar reflects a brief window of time during which a common assessment is administered and the date for your team to analyze the data. Once your team establishes a unit calendar and clarifies the essential learning standards with daily learning targets, it is ready to continue use of the Mathematics Unit Planner in figure 1.2 (page 11).

❸ Prior Knowledge

Which mathematics standards from a previous unit or grade level do students need to be successful in the current unit? How will you use prior-knowledge activities or mathematical tasks to remind students of their prior learning?

Your team identifies the prior-knowledge standards students require to access learning for each grade-level essential learning standard in the current unit. Which standard (or standards) that students learned most recently connects to the new required learning? For example, a team does not need to list *students can write numbers* when identifying a prerequisite skill for addition and subtraction within 100 in second grade. Instead, the team would focus on a more recent prerequisite skill that has a direct relationship to the skill students are currently learning. In this example, the second-grade team would reference addition and subtraction within 20 from first grade and an understanding of base ten with two-digit numbers.

Your team will use the prior-knowledge standards to create connection activities or mathematical tasks at the start of each lesson in the unit. Examples of such activities and tasks appear in *Mathematics Instruction and Tasks in a PLC at Work* (Kanold, Kanold-McIntyre, et al., 2018, p. 69). (Visit **go.SolutionTree.com/ MathematicsatWork** for free reproducibles.)

Figure 2.7 (page 25) is a template your team can use to identify prior-knowledge standards that support the essential learning standards for new learning in the unit. What is the mathematical trajectory of learning? How does this specific mathematics unit fit into the learning story for your students? The protocol ends with your team summarizing the prior-knowledge standard and providing an exemplar teachers can use later to determine prior-knowledge activities and tasks. PreK, kindergarten, first-, and second-grade examples of the prior-knowledge template related to foundations of addition and subtraction appear in figures 3.7 (page 50), 4.6 (page 71), 5.6 (page 94), and 6.6 (page 120).

Once your team identifies the prior knowledge from earlier standards to use as the driver for determining tasks to start lessons in the unit, you and your collaborative team are now ready to address the next part of the Mathematics Unit Planner: vocabulary and notations.

Team Unit Calendar

Directions: In the following calendar (or in a digital team calendar), identify dates in the unit for:

1. Starting and ending the unit

2. Administering any common mid-unit assessments and a common end-of-unit assessment

3. Analyzing data as a team from any common mid-unit and end-of-unit assessments to plan a team response to student learning

4. Deciding on essential learning standards the team will address each day of the unit to create a logical learning progression (identify the daily learning targets to address each day; teachers plan their own lessons for the targets aligning to the essential learning standards.)

5. Recording any holidays, professional development days, field trips, assemblies, or other events that might impact teaching the unit; clarifying as a team the most critical standards for student learning and emphasis throughout the unit

6. Identifying a possible flex day for teams to respond to student learning after a common mid-unit assessment

Monday	Tuesday	Wednesday	Thursday	Friday

Source: Adapted from Kanold & Schuhl, 2020, pp. 62–63.

Figure 2.6: Team discussion tool—unit calendar.

Visit go.SolutionTree.com/MathematicsatWork for a free reproducible version of this figure.

Directions: Use the standards from the previous grade levels or courses (or your current grade level or course standards) to determine the prior-knowledge standards students need to make connections to learning in the current unit. Summarize each prior-knowledge standard you identify, and provide an exemplar task. (Copy the state standards and essential learning standards into this template from the team protocol to unwrap and make sense of mathematics standards in figure 2.4, page 20.)

Unit: _____

Formal Unit Standards (State Standard Language)	Essential Learning Standards for Assessment and Reflection (Student-Friendly Language)	Prior-Knowledge Standards From Prior Grade Level, Course, or Unit	Prior-Knowledge Summary With an Exemplar
	I can . . .		
	I can . . .		
	I can . . .		
	I can . . .		
	I can . . .		

Figure 2.7: Protocol to determine prior knowledge for a mathematics unit.

Visit go.SolutionTree.com/MathematicsatWork for a free reproducible version of this figure.

❹ Vocabulary and Notations

The academic language of mathematics can be a stumbling block for students as they work to make sense of and learn each essential learning standard in a unit. In mathematics, academic language includes *vocabulary* (the meaning of words and abbreviations), and it includes *notations* (symbols) in the context of the essential learning standards (Kanold, Kanold-McIntyre, et al., 2018).

For each unit, your team must consider the academic vocabulary and notations students need to learn during lessons so they can engage in reading tasks, whole-group and small-group discussions, and writing to communicate their reasoning. According to Meir Ben-Hur (2006), senior international leader for the Feuerstein Institute, "Students who lack the formal language of mathematics have difficulties reasoning and communicating about mathematics" (p. 67). Emerging English learners also need to engage in mathematical discourse. Students learning English need opportunities to learn mathematics vocabulary, make conjectures, and explain their thinking (Civil & Turner, 2014).

With your team, identify the mathematics vocabulary words and symbols students need to precisely communicate and learn through their reading, writing, and discourse. Consider how students will learn the vocabulary and notations in real time through strong lesson design (see *Mathematics Instruction and Tasks in a PLC at Work* [Kanold, Kanold-McIntyre, et al., 2018, pp. 28–31]). (Visit **go.SolutionTree.com/MathematicsatWork** for free reproducibles.)

Figure 2.8 is a template for teams to document the mathematics academic vocabulary and notations students will learn in the current unit, as well as your team's shared understanding of the meaning and use of each notation or term. Find grade-level examples of vocabulary and notations in foundations of addition and subtraction units in figures 3.8 (page 51), 4.7 (page 72), 5.7 (page 96), and 6.7 (page 121).

Your grade-level primary team has now worked on a mathematics unit together to: (1) make sense of the essential learning standards, (2) create a unit calendar for learning and assessment, (3) identify the prior knowledge necessary for students to learn each essential learning standard, and (4) determine the mathematics vocabulary and notations students learn in the unit for communication and precision. Your team is now ready to identify resources and activities to teach the essential learning standards.

❺ Resources and Activities

When collaborative teams identify common resources and activities each member believes will effectively help every student learn the essential learning standards for the unit, each team member grows his or her own teacher efficacy.

For your preK, kindergarten, first-, and second-grade mathematics units, consider the following team actions.

- Determine examples of higher- and lower-level-cognitive-demand tasks (Smith & Stein, 1998) students need to demonstrate an ability to reason through or solve.
- Identify lessons and tasks in textbooks that support student learning.
- Identify online resources or alternate activities or projects to use with students to grow their understanding and application of procedural fluency with each essential learning standard.

At times, your team may create its own supplemental activities, and at other times, find them in resources or online.

Figure 2.9 (page 28) is a protocol and template to record team agreements on common resources and activities (including games) you can use to teach and assess student learning for each essential unit standard. Examples from preK, kindergarten, first-, and second-grade foundations of addition and subtraction units appear in figures 3.9 (page 53), 4.8 (page 74), 5.8 (page 99), and 6.8 (page 124). Record your team agreements in your Mathematics Unit Planner (see figure 1.2, page 11).

As your team identifies mathematics tasks, resources, projects, and activities for the unit, you should also create a list of tools and technology needed to help students learn the essential mathematics standards for the unit.

Directions: Determine the order students will learn key vocabulary and notations listed in the team protocol to unwrap and make sense of mathematics standards in figure 2.4 (page 20). As a team, identify academic mathematics vocabulary words students will learn in the unit, and clarify each word with the definition, an explanation, a drawing, or an example. Similarly, identify any mathematics notations students will learn, and clarify how to read and pronounce the symbols. Provide an example for how to use each notation mathematically in the unit.

Unit:		
Vocabulary	**Definition, Explanation, Drawing, or Example**	
Notation	**Words to Show How to Read the Notation**	**Example Showing How to Use the Notation in the Unit**

Figure 2.8: Protocol for mathematics vocabulary and notations.

Visit **go.SolutionTree.com/MathematicsatWork** *for a free reproducible version of this figure.*

Directions: Identify any mathematics tasks, resources, projects, and activities you could use to teach students each essential learning standard. Determine which ones, if any, members will use across the entire team for instructional purposes. As a team, verify each mathematics task, resource, project, or activity aligns with a state standard and the daily learning targets.

Essential Learning Standard	Lower-Level Task Example	Higher-Level Task Example	School-Adopted Textbook Lessons	Explorations, Projects, or Activities	Supplemental or Online Resources

Figure 2.9: Protocol for mathematics tasks, resources, projects, and activities.

Visit go.SolutionTree.com/MathematicsatWork for a free reproducible version of this figure.

❻ Tools and Technology

Teaching for conceptual understanding and procedural fluency requires students to learn using tools or manipulatives and technology. According to the National Research Council, students benefit from using physical objects during problem solving (Cross et al., 2009; Kilpatrick, Swafford, & Findell, 2001). They help young learners (and all learners) understand mathematical concepts to better understand the corresponding pictures and equations.

The use of tools and technology is also one of the guiding principles for school mathematics NCTM (2014a) identifies: "An excellent mathematics program integrates the use of mathematical tools and technology as essential resources to help students learn and make sense of mathematical ideas, reason mathematically, and communicate their mathematical thinking" (p. 5). However, be careful not to confuse tools with strategies. Tools are instruments used to *employ* a variety of mathematics strategies. Examples of tools include manipulatives or concrete objects, calculators, computers, paper and pencil, and a number line. Reserve your team conversations for tools to this part of the mathematics unit plan. In the last section of the plan, *Reflection and Notes*, your team can record any mathematical strategies members plan to use during the unit or did use that were most effective for student learning. Hands-on tools for students to use when making sense of mathematics, rather than technology, are often the focus in grades preK–2. Technology might include software games and online manipulatives or a calculator, as shown in the examples in chapters 3–6.

As a team, you determine the tools and technology needed to advance student understanding. Which tools are needed for your students at their grade- and knowledge-levels for them to engage in meaningful explorations that lead to conceptual understanding? Which are needed to advance understanding? Which are needed to support student learning? Discuss as a team how students will select the appropriate tools to use when solving problems during instruction and on assessments. Ultimately, recognize what materials and resources are available, and determine as a team which tools and technology students need to deeply learn each essential learning standard based on the materials and resources that are available to your students.

As you choose tools and technology for your students, keep in mind any tools or technology you may want to include from the tasks, resources, projects, and activities your team identified earlier. Use figure 2.10 (page 30) to identify the tools and technology you need in order to teach students the essential learning standards in a unit. Find grade-level examples of this protocol in figures 3.10 (page 54), 4.9 (page 76), 5.9 (page 100), and 6.9 (page 126).

The first six elements in the Mathematics Unit Planner (see figure 1.2, page 11) provide a framework for your team to use as you plan for common assessments and daily lessons. This next (and final) element provides space for your team to record any notes when teaching and reflection ideas to remember for next year.

❼ Reflection and Notes

As your team is planning a unit and completing the previously explained elements of unit planning, you may make decisions (such as mathematical strategies to emphasize or language to use) you want to remember when teaching the unit in the future. Enter these ideas and decisions in the last row of the Mathematics Unit Planner in figure 1.2 (page 11).

Furthermore, during and after the unit, your team should reflect (in writing) about the instructional and assessment routines that worked well for student learning, and you should identify changes for improvement in the future. According to NCTM (2014a), effective teachers collaboratively plan units, implement lessons, and then reflect on plans related to student learning in a cycle of continuous improvement. Recording your reflections in the last row of the Mathematics Unit Planner (see figure 1.2, page 11) allows your team to learn from the current year's experiences to better impact student learning of the essential learning standards in the same unit next year or in future units of the current year.

Use figure 2.11 (page 31) to document notes as your team plans and reflects on how to more effectively teach students the essential learning standards in the unit next year (or in the next unit). Grade-level examples showing foundations of addition and subtraction units are shared for preK in figure 3.11 (page 56), kindergarten in figure 4.10 (page 78), first grade in figure 5.10 (page 103), and second grade in figure 6.10 (page 128).

Directions: Determine any tools (including manipulatives) or technology (hardware and software) each student will use to learn the mathematics concepts and skills for the unit. Identify the purpose for each (such as conceptual understanding, exploration, application, or learning support). Decide which tools and technology you will use for instruction and which all team members will use for student common assessments during the unit.

Tool	Purpose	Instruction	Assessment

Technology	Purpose	Instruction	Assessment

Figure 2.10: Protocol for mathematics unit tools and technology.

Visit go.SolutionTree.com/MathematicsatWork for a free reproducible version of this figure.

Directions: (1) When planning the unit as a team, record any strategies or ideas you want all members to remember when teaching the essential learning standards, and (2) after the unit, determine as a team what worked well and what to replicate next year. Determine which aspects of the lessons and assessments your team needs to revise or change for the next school year or later in the current school year—for example, length of time spent on a lesson, revisions to common assessments, or use of a different strategy.

Essential Learning Standard	Notes When Planning: What to Emphasize or Remember for Lessons and Assessments in the Unit	Team Reflections After the Unit

Overall Unit Reflections: Things to Remember or Change for Next Year

Figure 2.11: Reflection and notes protocol for mathematics unit.

Visit go.SolutionTree.com/MathematicsatWork for a free reproducible version of this figure.

Visit **go.SolutionTree.com/MathematicsatWork** for a free reproducible version of this tool. See this book's epilogue (page 133) and figure E.1 (page 133) for how to organize your online files for each grade level. Your team's intentional unit planning creates equity across your grade level and collective responsibility for student learning during and after a mathematics unit of study. Use the protocols and tools from figure 1.2 (page 11) that you have learned about throughout this chapter to complete a mathematics unit plan for each unit of study at your grade level.

Find completed examples of foundations of addition and subtraction unit plans in figure 3.12 (page 58) for preK, figure 4.11 (page 79) for kindergarten, figure 5.11 (page 105) for first grade, and figure 6.11 (page 129) for second grade. Together these examples show a learning arc for foundations of addition and subtraction.

Use the "Team Checklist and Questions for Mathematics Unit Planning" (see appendix B, page 139) to evaluate current team progress related to planning quality units, and to spark team discussion related to each element of unit planning.

Planning your mathematics units as a collaborative team builds your teacher efficacy and confidence, grows student learning, and launches the work of your collaborative team. Your mathematics unit plans create your guaranteed and viable curriculum.

Part 2 of this book provides examples of mathematics units of study specific to many of the essential standards for foundations of addition and subtraction in grades preK–2. These protocols, tools, and models serve as exemplars to use in your team's planning, work, and efforts to help every student learn mathematics.

PART 2

Foundations of Addition and Subtraction
Unit Examples, Grades PreK–2

Patterning, decomposition, place value, and equivalence are all key ideas underlying an understanding of operations.

—Linda M. Platas

PART 2

Understanding the mathematics learning continuum along a trajectory (or story) arc helps your collaborative team identify the prior knowledge students need to access grade-level content, which, in turn, helps it understand how to prepare students for future learning experiences. Your team uses its knowledge of how standards tell a story that builds either vertically or horizontally, and throughout a year, it is able to better balance student learning through conceptual understanding, application, and procedural fluency. In *Adding It Up: Helping Children Learn Mathematics*, editors Jeremy Kilpatrick, Jane Swafford, and Bradford Findell (2001) write:

> Procedural fluency and conceptual understanding are often seen as competing for attention in school mathematics. But pitting skill against understanding creates a false dichotomy. Understanding makes learning skills easier, less susceptible to common errors, and less prone to forgetting. (p. 122)

The primary focus of learning foundations for addition and subtraction in the early childhood grades begins with counting in preK, composing and decomposing a ten in kindergarten, adding and subtracting to 20 in first grade using multiple strategies, and exploring multidigit addition and subtraction in second grade with an emphasis on place value. At each of these grade levels, much of the learning is rooted at the *conceptual understanding* level where students engage in building procedural fluency with developmentally appropriate concepts.

In preK, children are at an early stage of acquiring numeracy skills and begin to develop a solid foundation of counting concepts. Students learn counting principles and begin to build flexibility in thinking through various counting experiences. At this stage, students learn number recognition and how to count forward with numbers to 10. Engaging counting experiences through play and daily routines helps young children establish one-to-one correspondence, meaning to count objects with only one count per object.

One mathematics goal for preK students is to understand the counting principle of cardinality, where the last count indicates how many objects were counted. The concept of addition and subtraction is explored through joining and separating numbers within 5 in real problem contexts that students might encounter in their daily lives. The ability to subitize (instantly recognize small sets of dot images) is at the core of students developing an understanding of the part-whole relationship they need to operate with numbers.

Kindergarten students continue to build their counting skills and develop number concepts while starting to make sense of composing and decomposing numbers to ten (and later compose teen numbers as a ten and ones). They use anchor numbers such as 5 and 10, along with multiple representations and tools, to explore putting numbers together and taking numbers apart. Practical and engaging problem solving helps students make connections between the operations and their own personal experiences. Students are encouraged to reason and justify orally, with pictures, and with tools. Students in this grade level may still write reversals of single digits when recording their thinking and answers.

In kindergarten, your teacher team expects students to learn the essential mathematics skill of subitizing, which leads to recognizing how the sum of the individual parts creates a whole group or set. Use of dots or objects arranged on a five or ten frame and other regular patterns such as dot dice and rectangular arrangements develop this skill of recognizing quantities without counting. The use of the ten frame and fingers to compose and decompose ten begins each student's understanding of the base-ten system and, therefore, is foundational to learning in the early grades.

By first grade, students start to connect their concrete experiences with composing and decomposing numbers and use these connections to learn basic facts of addition and subtraction, and they apply this understanding of basic facts to the use of more efficient strategies such as counting on or using a ten. By the end of the school year, students are expected to interpret a variety of contexts involving joining, separating, comparing, and part-part-whole relationships. First graders begin to explore the concept of equality as they grapple with unknowns in various positions and represent problems with equations. Students may even start to notice patterns and begin to generalize rules for addition or subtraction or even apply properties like the commutative and associative properties of addition.

Students in second grade work toward *procedural fluency*, meaning they develop efficient and effective strategies for adding and subtracting with numbers to 20. While second-grade students are becoming more efficient with basic facts, they are at the earliest stages of understanding multidigit computation. Therefore, a second grader's experiences in operating with larger numbers must be grounded in place value and built on a foundation of the base-ten system. Students use concrete and pictorial models to compose and decompose numbers to 1,000. Students apply their understanding of composing and decomposing a ten to add and subtract within 100. In second grade, students continue to be exposed to complex single-step practical problems but are also, for the first time, exploring two-step problems as well. Care is taken to make sure students can record and organize their thinking and reasoning on paper using pictures and equations.

Armed with knowledge about *how* the mathematics foundations of addition and subtraction story of learning grows across grade levels and within a grade level, your preK, kindergarten, first-, or second-grade collaborative team can better plan for student learning of number sense and operations.

Chapters 3–6 in part 2 show specific examples for *how* your grade-level team could use each teacher team discussion protocol from part 1 (page 5) to plan a mathematics unit related to foundations of addition and subtraction. Specifically, part 2 focuses on a sample set of standards related to foundations of addition and subtraction from preK, kindergarten, first, and second grade as illustrated in table P2.1. As noted, standards in the early grades are often spiraled. Therefore, the units in part 2 may come before or after other units that also include counting, place value, addition, and subtraction, to deepen a student's understanding of each.

In the table, bold standards represent the need-to-know standards and those remaining are the important-to-know standards (see figure 2.3, page 19) for each unit.

Throughout chapters 3–6, you will find examples of the reasoning and decision making a grade-level team uses to generate meaningful and relevant mathematical learning experiences for students in a unit. The unit-planning models show a learning trajectory (or arc) and tell a story about starting from students in preK understanding counting, joining, and separating numbers to students in preK and kindergarten subitizing and composing a 10 to students in first and second grade developing fact fluency to, finally, students in second grade building a foundation for addition and subtraction with regrouping.

Table P2.1: Grades PreK–2 Mathematics Standards for Foundations of Addition and Subtraction Units

| PreK
Counting and Cardinality | Kindergarten
Addition and Subtraction to 10 | First Grade
Addition and Subtraction to 20 | Second Grade
Multidigit Addition and Subtraction |
|---|---|---|---|
| **PK.1. Know number names and rote counting sequence from 1–10.**

PK.2. Recognize the numerals 0–9 and orally say the number that the numeral represents.

PK.3. Count a set of 1–10 objects with one-to-one correspondence (one count and number name per object).

PK.4. Understand that the last count indicates how many objects were counted.

PK.5. Use subitizing to identify the number of objects in a set of 5 or less (for example, images on dot dice, five frame, and other dot arrangements).

PK.6. Use concrete objects, pictorial models, and/or verbal problem contexts for joining and separating up to 5 objects. | **K.1. Use subitizing to instantly recognize a quantity of 1–10 using dot dice, five and ten frames, and other dot arrangements.**

K.2. Compose and decompose numbers less than or equal to 10 in more than one way using objects, drawings, fingers, and verbal expressions (for example, 5 is 3 and 2 or 4 and 1).

K.3. Represent various verbal problem contexts involving joining and separating numbers to 10.

K.4. For any number from 1 to 9, find the number that makes 10 when added to the given number (for example, by using objects or drawings) and record the answer with a drawing or equation. | **1.1. Fluently compose and decompose 10 with and without objects and pictures.**

1.2. Apply basic fact strategies to add and subtract within 20, including counting on, making 10 and decomposing a number leading to a 10, and using the relationship between addition and subtraction.

1.3. Use addition and subtraction within 20 to solve word problems that involve joining, separating, comparing, and part-whole relationships with the unknowns in all positions.

1.4. Determine the unknown whole number in an addition or subtraction equation relating three whole numbers. For example, 4 + ? = 13, 8 = ☐ − 3, 3 + 3 = ? | **2.1. Fluently add and subtract within 20 using mental strategies leading to immediate recall.**

2.2. Use concrete and pictorial models to represent numbers up to 1,000 in more than one way as sums of hundreds, tens, and ones.

2.3. Estimate and find multidigit sums and differences within 100, with and without regrouping, using various methods based on place value.

2.4. Use addition and subtraction within 100 to represent and solve one- and two-step word problems involving joining, separating, comparing, and part-whole relationships with the unknowns in all positions. |

CHAPTER 3

PreK Unit: Counting and Cardinality

Children begin forming counting and early numeracy understanding before entering the school setting. In preK, it is important to ensure student learning occurs through play and real-, home-, and school-life routines because learning is not accidental. For example, numeracy skills are built when a student plays a board game and counts spaces using a number card, spinner, or dots on a die, or when a student counts how many apple slices are on a plate for snack. Instead of just picking up toys at the end of the day, students might be asked to pick up five toys or be asked which student picked up the most toys in the class so students can compare. It takes intentional planning to create meaningful play opportunities that lead to students acquiring numeracy concepts and skills.

The counting sequence, number identification, subitizing, and counting to tell how many are in a group are foundational skills to a student's addition and subtraction story in the early primary grades. In preK, children begin to develop the rote counting sequence and attach meaning to numerals and quantities. Students further develop counting principles in kindergarten where they more formally explore joining and separating problem contexts and learn to count on from a number. Then, in first and second grade, students use their understanding of composing and decomposing numbers and place value in base-ten to add and subtract numbers with regrouping to 20 and 100 and with special cases to 1,000.

While this chapter outlines a unit containing essential counting standards for preK, teachers and teams should integrate counting throughout the entire school year. The range of numbers might include up to five in the fall, to ten by late winter, and possibly beyond ten for some students by spring. The skills this unit highlights could be a continuation of previously taught skills because children need plenty of experiences and practice over long periods of time to develop mastery.

This chapter shares examples of how your prekindergarten mathematics team could plan for a *counting and cardinality* unit. The standards that follow may or may not match your exact state standards, but most likely contain the key ideas for most of your local district standards. The state standards related to counting used in this unit are the same as those in table P2.1 (page 37) and are labeled *standards PK.1–PK.6*.

PK.1. Know number names and rote counting sequence from 1–10.

PK.2. Recognize the numerals 0–9 and orally say the number that the numeral represents.

PK.3. Count a set of 1–10 objects with one-to-one correspondence (one count and number name per object).

PK.4. Understand that the last count indicates how many objects were counted.

PK.5. Use subitizing to identify the number of objects in a set of 5 or less (for example, images on dot dice, five frame, and other dot arrangements).

PK.6. Use concrete objects, pictorial models, and/or verbal problem contexts for joining and separating up to 5 objects.

The bold standards reflect the need-to-know essential standards in the unit (see figure 2.3, page 19). These are the standards your team uses when creating common mid-unit assessments for monitoring student learning, and they are what your team uses first when addressing student gaps or extensions in learning. Your team locates these more critical standards for the unit in district documents or state, provincial, or national guidelines. The bold standards are not, however, the only standards students will learn in the unit. The standards not in bold are the important-to-know standards included on your common end-of-unit assessment.

The distinction between the two types of standards in the unit is that the bold (need-to-know) standards are critical for all future learning in the primary grades and most students have, at the very least, informal exposure to counting and numeracy ideas prior to coming to school. Therefore, it is appropriate to expect preK mastery over these counting skills and concepts by the end of the year. However, solving problems by joining and separating objects and subitizing quantities (ability to recognize structured dot and object arrangements without counting) will continue in kindergarten, with an expectation for proficiency at that time, and so they are of less critical importance at the preK level than are the need-to-know standards.

Once your team has clarity about the standards in the unit and how they fit in the foundations of addition and subtraction story arc of a student in preK, it is time to begin creating your unit plan. The Mathematics Unit Planner will guide your team and provide a location to record your team agreements (see figure 1.2, page 11). Your team's work starts with generating essential learning standards in student-friendly language for assessment and reflection.

❶ Essential Learning Standards

The essential learning standards are the driver for common assessments team members use throughout the unit, and they support the decisions you make about student learning experiences. They are written as *I can* statements and generated from the state standards students must learn in the unit. They form the daily learning targets for lessons.

What *exactly* do students have to know and be able to do to be proficient with the standards in the unit? What does your team understand about the counting principles and the way children develop numeracy? Together, the members of your team can use the team protocol

in figure 2.4 (page 20) to unwrap and make sense of mathematics standards. Completed templates for the need-to-know standards of the unit appear in figures 3.1, 3.2 (page 42), 3.3 (page 43), and 3.4 (page 45).

In standard PK.1 (figure 3.1), students are learning to count, but they may not yet understand that each number represents a different quantity. Much like reciting the alphabet without understanding each letter, students are perhaps memorizing the language of counting to 10.

Similarly, in standard PK.2 (figure 3.2, page 42), students are learning to recognize numbers (some students confuse numerals and letters in their quest to recognize both, so you may have to help students distinguish numbers from letters). Students identify a numeral when the teacher gives the name of a numeral or shows the student a set that matches the numeral. Students also say the name of the number when the teacher shows its numeral. The unwrapped standard PK.2 appears in figure 3.2 (page 42).

During the process of unwrapping a standard, it might be helpful to consider how students are expected to show proficiency of each standard on a common assessment or by the end of the year. A common formative observation tool or checklist can be used to reassess learning over time, serve as a record of progress, and identify which skills students have not yet mastered. Having a clear picture of the end goal can support your preK team as you generate ideas and navigate conversations that lead to being ready to complete the components of the unwrapping protocol.

The counting checklists in the exemplar tasks section include a column for when and if a student goes beyond the benchmark or suggests a choice of number that may be outside the preK range. It isn't uncommon for your preK students to have a wide range in abilities and prior experiences when it comes to counting. Being able to articulate with which skill and to what degree a student is performing below, at, or above grade level will help support your team's thinking when planning to differentiate instruction or provide interventions.

Standard PK.3 (figure 3.3, page 43) extends the learning from PK.1 and PK.2. Students do not just count or recognize and name numerals, but they begin to understand the meaning of numbers.

Standards PK.3 in figure 3.3 (page 43) and PK.4 in figure 3.4 (page 45) are interconnected concepts

Unit: PreK—Counting and Cardinality

State Standard in the Unit:

PK.1. (Know) number names and <u>rote counting sequence from 1–10</u>.

Conceptual Understanding What do students need to know?	Procedural Knowledge and Skills What do students need to do?
• Number names 1–10 • Rote counting sequence 1–10	• Orally say names of numbers 1–10. • Orally count 1–10 using the rote pattern or sequence of the numbers.

Academic Vocabulary and Notations			
Number	Two	Five	Eight
Count	Three	Six	Nine
One	Four	Seven	Ten

Essential Learning Standard

(In student-friendly language—I can . . .)

• I can count from 1 to 10.

Proficiency Level of Understanding	
4 **Advanced**	Say the number names during a rote count in the correct sequence from 1 to a number greater than 10.
3 **Proficient**	Say the number names during a rote count in the correct sequence from 1 to 10 without errors or recount.
2 **Partial**	Say the number names during a rote count in the correct sequence from 1 to 5, but may recount, have sequence error, or omit numbers after 5 and up to 10.
1 **Minimal**	Say very few number names during a rote count without inaccuracies in the sequence from 1 to 5.

Exemplar Tasks to Meet Standard:

Task 1—Active Counting

Clap, stomp, or step during the rote counting pattern of numbers 1 through 10.

Task 2—Counting Checklist

Student Names	Count to 5 With Prompts or Errors	Count to 5 No Prompts or Errors	Count to 10 With Prompts or Errors	Count to 10 No Prompts or Errors	Count Beyond 10 (Record Highest Number)	Notes and Observations

Figure 3.1: Unwrap and make sense of standard PK.1.

Unit: PreK—Counting and Cardinality

State Standard in the Unit:

PK.2. Recognize the numerals 0–9 and orally say the number that the numeral represents.

Conceptual Understanding What do students need to know?	Procedural Knowledge and Skills What do students need to do?
• Numerals 0–9 • Number names 0–9	• Recognize numerals 0–9. • Orally say the numbers 0–9 when given a numeral 0–9.

Academic Vocabulary and Notations						
Number	0 (Zero)	1 (One)	2 (Two)	3 (Three)	4 (Four)	5 (Five)	6 (Six)
7 (Seven)	8 (Eight)	9 (Nine)					

Essential Learning Standard (In student-friendly language—I can . . .)
• I know numbers and can say the names.

Proficiency Level of Understanding	
4 **Advanced**	Recognize the numerals 0–9, and greater, in any order.
3 **Proficient**	Recognize the numerals 0–9 with minimal errors or may need to count from 1 to say the numeral.
2 **Partial**	Recognize some of the numerals 0–9, but not all. May be able to select a numeral from a choice of 2 or 3 when the teacher says the number.
1 **Minimal**	Cannot yet recognize more than one or two numerals 0–9.

Exemplar Tasks to Meet Standard:

Task 1—Number Hunt

Students can circle or point to a number after being given a prompt such as, "Can you find all of the eights?"

Task 2—Number Card

Show students a card with a numeral, and ask them to say the number shown.

5	7	1	2

Task 3—Roll and Say

Students take turns rolling a ten-sided die or large foam ten-sided die showing numerals 0 to 9 and say the number shown on the ten-sided die.

Task 4—Numeral Identification Checklist

Use cards with numerals, observations from classroom activities, or ten-sided dice to determine which numerals students can identify. Record the student results in the following checklist.

Student	0	1	2	3	4	5	6	7	8	9	Multidigit Numbers	Notes and Observations

Figure 3.2: Unwrap and make sense of standard PK.2.

Unit: PreK—Counting and Cardinality	

State Standard in the Unit:

PK.3. (Count) a set of 1–10 objects with one-to-one correspondence (one count and number name per object).

Conceptual Understanding What do students need to know?	Procedural Knowledge and Skills What do students need to do?
• Set of 1–10 objects • One-to-one correspondence • One object per count and number name	• Count and say one object per count (one-to-one correspondence). • Stay organized and keep track while counting a set of tangible objects. • Move or touch objects to correspond with the count.

Academic Vocabulary and Notations	
Count	Six
One	Seven
Two	Eight
Three	Nine
Four	Ten
Five	

Essential Learning Standard (In student-friendly language—I can . . .)	

• I can count objects.

(For example, I can count crackers; I can count blocks.)

Proficiency Level of Understanding	
4 **Advanced**	Counts ten or more objects independently and has a working system for keeping track of the count. Or, may use a more advanced counting strategy such as grouping and counting by 2s.
3 **Proficient**	Counts ten objects independently, but needs objects in a line or other scaffolds for keeping track of the count.
2 **Partial**	Counts a smaller set of objects (at least five) independently with or without scaffolds.
1 **Minimal**	Counts and keeps track of the count even with numbers 5 or less with support from the teacher (for example, choral teacher and student counting with hand-over-hand support).

Figure 3.3: Unwrap and make sense of standard PK.3.

continued →

Exemplar Tasks to Meet Standard:

Task 1—How Many?

Place a set of objects on the table (like cubes, bears, or toy cars). Ask the student to give you an amount. For example, "Give me 8 bears." The student is expected to count out 8 bears and hand them to the teacher.

Task 2—Counting Collections

Prepare a variety of objects for students to count that are easy to pick up and move, such as cubes, bears, and toy cars. Select a number appropriate for the learner: 4, 7, 10, 15, and so on. Use the questions in the following tasks for correspondence and cardinality, and record student results using the following checklist.

1–1 Correspondence:		Cardinality:	
Student says the number names in order, pairing each object with one number name and each number name with one and only one object.		Student understands that when counting a set, the last number represents the total number of the objects in the set.	
Correspondence Task: Ask the student to count a set of cubes (for example, "Count seven cubes").		Cardinality Task: Using the same set of seven cubes, ask the student, "How many did you just count?"	
Observation:		Observation:	
Does the student have a system for keeping track of the objects?		If the student has cardinality, he or she will tell you the amount immediately. If the student doesn't, he or she will have to recount the cubes repeatedly.	
Does the student count each object only once?			
Does the student touch and count? Move objects to stay organized?			
Student	Number Used	1–1 Correspondence	Cardinality
		☐ Yes ☐ No	☐ Yes ☐ No
		Observations:	Observations:
		☐ Yes ☐ No	☐ Yes ☐ No
		Observations:	Observations:
		☐ Yes ☐ No	☐ Yes ☐ No
		Observations:	Observations:

Unit: PreK—Counting and Cardinality	
State Standard in the Unit: PK.4. Understand that the last count indicates how many objects were counted.	

Conceptual Understanding **What do students need to know?**	Procedural Knowledge and Skills **What do students need to do?**
• The last number in the count names the amount or how many objects	• Understand that the last number said indicates the amount of objects counted (cardinality). • Count a group of objects.

Academic Vocabulary and Notations					
Count	One	Two	Three	Four	Five
Six	Seven	Eight	Nine	Ten	

Essential Learning Standard (In student-friendly language—I can . . .)
• I can say how many I counted.

Proficiency Level of Understanding	
4 **Advanced**	Indicates the number of objects counted and does not recount (even when the objects are covered or concealed) when asked, "How many did we just count?"
3 **Proficient**	Indicates the number of objects counted and does not recount (while the set of objects remains in view) when asked, "How many did we just count?"
2 **Partial**	Inconsistently indicates the number of objects counted and when asked, "How many did we just count?" needs to count the objects a second time.
1 **Minimal**	Cannot yet indicate the number of objects counted and repeatedly recounts the set.

Exemplar Tasks to Meet Standard:

Task 1—Counting at Snack Time

Routinely using snack time to reinforce the number sequence and the concept of cardinality engages students in counting for an authentic purpose. Presenting a small quantity of crackers, the teacher can encourage students to count and then ask, "How many crackers did we just count?"

Task 2—Clean-Up Count

Counting while putting blocks back into a container, stacking cups to put on a shelf, or placing crayons into a pencil box sets students up for a similarly purposeful experience. Each time the teacher can ask, "How many did we put away?"

(See also assessment checklist in figure 3.3.)

Figure 3.4: Unwrap and make sense of standard PK.4.

and not taught or assessed in isolation. Therefore, Task 2—Counting Collections in figure 3.3 provides a scenario where the teacher is formatively assessing both one-to-one correspondence (PK.3) and cardinality (PK.4) during the same observation. A student's level of proficiency for these two standards depends on the number being used and whether the student requires prompts or scaffolds. In kindergarten, a student, given objects in a circle or placed randomly, will know when to stop counting if he or she understands that a number tells how many. If he or she only has one-to-one correspondence, the student will continue to count objects around the circle until he or she runs out of known numbers.

A student's proficiency with the rote counting sequence, standard PK.1 (see figure 3.1, page 41), impacts your choice of number to be used during the counting observation. For students struggling to count, you might start with numbers to 2 and then over time grow the numbers to 5 and eventually to 10. You might also start with more common numbers such as 0, 1, 2, 5, and 10. These will be discussions for your team to engage in to best meet the needs of each student. Thus, during the unwrapping process, it is important to keep in mind the connections between these standards.

Standards PK.1–PK.4 are the need-to-know standards in this counting and cardinality unit. Your team will similarly need to build a shared understanding of the remaining important-to-know standards in the unit—standards PK.5 and PK.6. Once complete, your preK mathematics team can combine the information to generate the counting and cardinality unit essential learning standards and daily learning targets (see figure 3.5). (See figure 2.5, page 22, for the template with directions.)

The *I can* statements (in the center column of figure 3.5) show the essential learning standards for the counting and cardinality unit. These statements are written so that students can communicate their learning, but also so your team can provide parent-friendly descriptions of the unit content to share in home communication or newsletters. Your team writes these essential learning standards in the first row of the Mathematics Unit Planner for preK counting and cardinality (see figure 3.12, page 58).

Both the essential learning standards and daily learning targets provide resources for your team as you plan lessons, mathematics stations or centers, and assessment opportunities. The next step for team unit planning is to add the dates for common assessments to the calendar and create the learning story with daily learning targets.

❷ Unit Calendar

The unit calendar includes common assessment dates and the student-friendly targets that help shape the story of learning that is about to take place. This calendar is not meant to be a lockstep approach to teaching among team members. Rather, the goal is to have an idea of how long to spend on each essential learning standard and the general order of when to address learning targets.

Intentionally including time in the unit to connect current learning to prior learning is just one consideration to keep in mind when developing the unit calendar. A preK team is likely to discuss which targets are connected, and therefore taught together. For young students, teachers often gather assessment information through observations (ongoing assessments). Whether observing a child during play and using a checklist to note important observations or conducting an interview with a set of predetermined questions, both scenarios are intentional or planned and take considerable time to complete. Determining when to give the common mid-unit assessments as part of an ongoing common benchmark or as a stand-alone assessment for the need-to-know standards helps not only govern the pace of the lessons but also ensures that gathering evidence of student learning is a priority among all team members and an ongoing process in preK.

An example of a team-developed calendar for preK appears in figure 3.6 (page 48). The calendar articulates the time line of learning targets, common assessment dates, and important events (such as holidays or teacher workdays) so that the team has a solid picture of how much instructional time is available and how they will use it. Your team may want to include a flex day mid-unit to reteach a concept, but most likely in preK, your team will use mini-lessons for that purpose and include multiple days for learning each target so there is time to address learning gaps in those mini-lessons.

The example depicts a third-quarter unit, and therefore not the first counting unit of the year. Counting units spiral throughout the school year and may be unique in the range of numbers used, the depth of the standards, and the themes explored. This repetition strengthens students' understanding of number. Often, teachers use routines throughout the year so students have already been addressing concepts such as counting, number identification, and subitizing.

If this is the first time your team is making a calendar, start with identifying the dates of your agreed-on common assessments in the unit. Next, work together as a team to plan the flow of the unit, but understand that through the reflection during each unit, the flow and storyline will become stronger and more precise each year.

Formal Unit Standards (State Standard Language)	Essential Learning Standards for Assessment and Reflection (Student-Friendly Language)	Daily Learning Targets — What students must know and be able to do for each lesson (unwrapped standards) (Storyboard Progression)
PK.1. Know number names and rote counting sequence from 1–10.	• I can count from 1 to 10.	Students will be able to: • Orally say names of numbers 1–10 • Orally count 1–10 using the rote pattern or sequence of the numbers
PK.2. Recognize the numerals 0–9 and orally say the number that the numeral represents.	• I know numbers and can say the names.	Students will be able to: • Recognize numerals 0–9 • Orally say the numbers 0–9 when given a numeral 0–9
PK.3. Count a set of 1–10 objects with one-to-one correspondence (one count and number name per object).	• I can count objects.	Students will be able to: • Count and say one object per count (one-to-one correspondence) • Stay organized and keep track while counting a set of tangible objects • Move or touch objects to correspond with the count
PK.4. Understand that the last count indicates how many objects were counted.	• I can say how many I counted.	Students will be able to: • Understand that the last number said indicates the amount of objects counted (cardinality) • Count a group of objects
PK.5. Use subitizing to identify the number of objects in a set of 5 or less (for example, images on dot dice, five frame, and other dot arrangements).	• I can say how many dots I see without counting.	Students will be able to: • Instantly recognize the number of dots without counting from one
PK.6. Use concrete objects, pictorial models, and/or verbal problem contexts for joining and separating up to 5 objects.	• I can solve story problems.	Students will be able to: • Join up to five objects in a verbal story context • Separate up to five objects in a verbal story context

Figure 3.5: PreK counting and cardinality unit standards, essential learning standards, and daily learning targets.

Monday	Tuesday	Wednesday	Thursday	Friday
3/2 Routine: Subitize dot images Lesson: Rote Counting and Count a Set of Objects	3/3 Routine: Subitize dot images Lesson: Rote Counting and Count a Set of Objects	3/4 Routine: Subitize dot images Lesson: Rote Counting and Count a Set of Objects	3/5 Routine: Subitize dot images Lesson: Rote Counting and Count a Set of Objects	3/6 Routine: Subitize dot images Lesson: Rote Counting and Count a Set of Objects
3/9 Routine: Subitize dot images Lesson: Rote Counting and Count a Set of Objects	3/10 **Common Ongoing Assessment:** • I can count objects. • I can count from 1 to 10.	3/11 **Common Ongoing Assessment:** • I can count objects. • I can count from 1 to 10.	3/12 Routine: Chant counting to 10 Lesson: Count a Set of Objects and Number Names	3/13 Routine: Chant counting to 10 Lesson: Count a Set of Objects and Number Names
3/16 Teacher Workday No School for Students	3/17 Routine: Chant counting to 10 Lesson: Count a Set of Objects and Number Names	3/18 Routine: Chant counting to 10 Lesson: Count a Set of Objects and Number Names	3/19 Routine: Chant counting to 10 Lesson: Count a Set of Objects and Number Names	3/20 Routine: Chant counting to 10 Lesson: Count a Set of Objects and Number Names
3/23 **Common Ongoing Assessment:** • I can count objects. • I can say how many I counted. • I know numbers and can say the names.	3/24 **Common Ongoing Assessment:** • I can count objects. • I can say how many I counted. • I know numbers and can say the names.	3/25 Routine: Subitize dot images Lesson: Story Problems With Totals to 5	3/26 Routine: Subitize dot images Lesson: Story Problems With Totals to 5	3/27 Routine: Count a set of objects Lesson: Story Problems With Totals to 5
3/30 Routine: Count a set of objects Lesson: Story Problems With Totals to 5	3/31 Routine: Number names Lesson: Story Problems With Totals to 5	4/1 **Common End-of-Unit Assessment:** • I can count from 1 to 10. • I know numbers and can say the names. • I can count objects. • I can say how many I counted. • I can say how many dots I see without counting. • I can solve story problems.	4/2 **Common End-of-Unit Assessment:** • I can count from 1 to 10. • I know numbers and can say the names. • I can count objects. • I can say how many I counted. • I can say how many dots I see without counting. • I can solve story problems.	4/3 **Common End-of-Unit Assessment:** • I can count from 1 to 10. • I know numbers and can say the names. • I can count objects. • I can say how many I counted. • I can say how many dots I see without counting. • I can solve story problems.

Figure 3.6: PreK counting and cardinality unit calendar.

If your preK team decides dates need to change during a unit, it is important to communicate the possible changes with all members. Consult your proficiency map or yearlong pacing guide to ensure you still have time for the remaining units. Record any changes in the Reflection and Notes portion of the Mathematics Unit Planner (see figure 1.2, page 11) to remember them for the next year.

Once your team has an agreed-on calendar and storyline for the unit, the next step is to discuss the prior knowledge members expect students to be proficient with before the unit of instruction begins. Sometimes in preK you will not expect any prior knowledge; however, since this unit is in the third quarter, you can ask, "What did students learn earlier this year for them to better make sense of the counting expectations in this unit?"

❸ Prior Knowledge

PreK is unique for many reasons, one of which is that for many students, it is their first formal schooling. There are vast differences in the prior learning experiences among toddlers and preschoolers, and therefore teams might consider doing some shared learning around numeracy development and how students grow in their understanding of number from first introduction to being able to add and subtract.

Organizations such as the National Association for the Education of Young Children (NAEYC) provide resources and research that can help educators understand how counting develops in young children. In later units during the year, such as this unit in the third quarter, teams might also consider the prior knowledge students learned in units earlier during the school year.

Once your team identifies prior-knowledge state standards for each essential learning standard in the unit, consider summarizing each one so it is friendly to read in the Mathematics Unit Planner (see figure 1.2, page 11). The far-right column in figure 3.7 (page 50) matches the prior-knowledge standards in the preK counting and cardinality unit planner (see figure 3.12, page 58). (See figure 2.7, page 25, for the template with directions.)

As each teacher on your preK team designs lessons, you can connect prior knowledge to the day's learning target through your use of an intentional task, routine, or activity. You might start lessons by incorporating number routines that develop counting skills. Teachers may use tasks that connect to the day's learning target and support the development of necessary prerequisite skills, as Kanold, Kanold-McIntyre, et al. (2018) discuss in *Mathematics Instruction and Tasks in a PLC at Work*. (Visit **go.SolutionTree.com/MathematicsatWork** for free reproducibles.)

Your team has now articulated the essential standards and identified the prior knowledge students will use to make connections to new learning. Next, your team determines the mathematics language students are expected to understand and use when counting.

❹ Vocabulary and Notations

Students are expected to interpret and use the language of mathematics as they demonstrate mastery of certain standards. With young children, vocabulary instruction includes connecting language (number words) to the symbols (numerals) and the visual models (objects and pictures) that help a child make meaning (Lesh, Post, & Behr, 1987).

Teachers often support language development in a preK classroom by using songs, poems, and books in an effort to use repetition so students hear, say, and see words and numbers many times. Teacher teams can generate lists of engaging literature, take pictures of anchor charts and visuals, and electronically archive working ideas that contribute not only to vocabulary development but to the instructional plan for mathematics. Adding to and refining this list is an ongoing part of team reflection. In *Mathematics Instruction and Tasks in a PLC at Work* (Kanold, Kanold-McIntyre, et al., 2018), there are several ideas for how to infuse the learning of academic vocabulary and notations into daily lessons as a component of quality lesson design.

Figure 3.8 (page 51) shows a team protocol for determining the meaning of each academic vocabulary word needed to build numeracy language in preK. (See figure 2.8, page 27, for the template with directions.) List the words and notations (if any) in the counting and cardinality unit planner (see figure 3.12, page 58). The right column of the vocabulary part will most likely include pictures and visuals to explain the meaning of each vocabulary word for students since students are not yet readers.

Formal Unit Standards (State Standard Language)	Essential Learning Standards for Assessment and Reflection (Student-Friendly Language)	Prior-Knowledge Standards From Prior Grade Level, Course, or Unit	Prior-Knowledge Summary With Exemplars
PK.1. Know number names and rote counting sequence from 1–10.	• I can count from 1 to 10.	**PreK:** Know number names and rote counting sequence for numbers to 5.	• Count from 1 to 5. Routinely count to 5 during play, songs, and in books.
PK.2. Recognize the numerals 0–9 and orally say the number that the numeral represents.	• I know numbers and can say the names.	**PreK:** Recognize numerals to 5.	• Recognize numerals to 5. Given two choices, student can point to the correct number given orally that is 5 or less.
PK.3. Count a set of 1–10 objects with one-to-one correspondence (one count and number name per object).	• I can count objects.	**PreK:** Count a set of 1 to 5 objects with one count per object. Objects that are few in number and arranged in a straight line are most appropriate for early counting experiences.	• Count a set of 1 to 5 objects (one-to-one correspondence). Count crackers during snack time or toy cars during play.
PK.4. Understand that the last count indicates how many objects were counted.	• I can say how many I counted.	**PreK:** Count a set of 1 to 5 objects with one count per object.	• Count a set of 1 to 5 objects (cardinality). Count when going up a small set of stairs. Ask, "How many stairs did we climb?"
PK.5. Use subitizing to identify the number of objects in a set of 5 or less (for example, images on dot dice, five frame, and other dot arrangements).	• I can say how many dots I see without counting.	**PreK:** Identify single-dot images no larger than three. Count a set of 1 to 5 picture models with one count per object.	• Subitize 1 to 3 dots. Show a dot card with up to 3 dots, and students identify the number of dots without counting.
PK.6. Use concrete objects, pictorial models, and/or verbal problem contexts for joining and separating up to 5 objects.	• I can solve story problems.	**PreK:** Join and separate up to 3 objects during real-life contexts and settings.	• Join and separate up to 3 objects to model story problems. [Child's name] has 2 cookies and gets 1 more cookie. How many cookies are there in all? [Child's name] has 1 red block and 1 blue block. How many blocks are there in all?

Figure 3.7: Prior-knowledge standards for preK counting and cardinality unit.

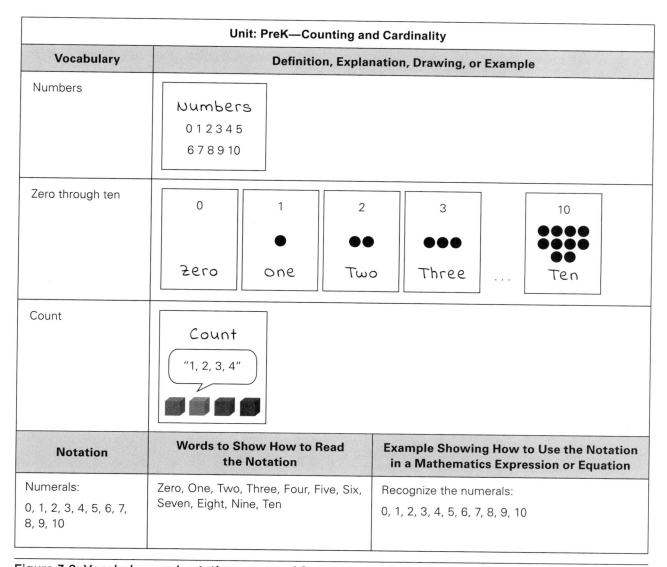

Figure 3.8: Vocabulary and notations protocol for preK counting and cardinality unit.

Your preK team may also want to participate in a vertical dialogue with kindergarten, first-, and second-grade teams about vocabulary that connects curriculum year to year. Together, your teams can determine common visuals, definitions, and displays that support counting and cardinality.

The next component of the unit planner outlines the instructional resources and activities that your team might use in the classroom. Determining key resources and activities as a team is central for delivering a guaranteed and viable curriculum to all learners.

❺ Resources and Activities

Developing a strong sense of number, understanding the patterns of the forward counting sequence, and subitizing dot images are foundational to a student's

ability to work with addition and subtraction in future grades. What are the best types of cognitive-demand tasks, both higher level and lower level, to develop conceptual understanding, application, and procedural fluency? How can your preK team develop a repertoire of play-based activities that are both developmentally appropriate and engaging to learners? As a preK collaborative team, you can work together to identify any common resources or activities that will effectively help every student learn the grade-level essential learning standards.

Once your team has clarity on the essential learning standards and examples of mathematical tasks to use for instruction and assessment, it is time to consider your resources. Your team might consider the following questions.

- Which parts of our school-adopted textbook or program correlate to the standards in the unit?

- Which are the best lessons or tasks to use in our books or program?

- Are there lessons or tasks to omit because they don't match the standards in the unit?

- What ongoing centers or learning stations should we prepare to include?

- What additional explorations, activities, or lessons are needed to teach each essential learning standard? What other resources should we use or develop?

Figure 3.9 shows possible answers to the preceding questions and examples of lower- and higher-level-cognitive-demand tasks for the essential learning standards in the unit. (See figure 2.9, page 28, for the template with directions.) Some parts of the chart might be blank because, for example, your preK team may decide no supplemental or online resources are necessary or available. If a textbook series or program is not available to your preK team, you could consider referencing the kindergarten textbook or program for lessons, activities, and teacher language ideas that could be adapted to align with preK standards.

As your preK team selects a balance of high- and low-level-cognitive-demand tasks that match the rigor proficient students demonstrate, you are contributing to a shared bank of resources. Additionally, team members may prepare learning stations or play activities that are interest based and allow for student choice. It is here—in the selection of resources—that the most significant teacher learning occurs, as your team archives what to use for instruction from year to year. Your resources should be intentionally kept, adjusted, or discarded based on the evidence of student learning you and your team collect.

One of the remaining elements of the Mathematics Unit Planner (see figure 1.2, page 11) is Tools and Technology. Your team has likely already been discussing tools and technology through your previous conversations related to unit planning thus far. The Tools and Technology part of the Mathematics Unit Planner provides a location for your team to document your decisions, whether at this point in planning or throughout your team's unit planning process.

❻ Tools and Technology

Learning mathematics in early childhood means using a variety of concrete manipulatives, toys, and everyday objects, all of which can be mathematical tools. Tools are instruments used to support specific strategies and learning outcomes. Some examples include using five and ten frames to organize a count and start to build an understanding of five and ten as anchor numbers. Students use concrete representations to make sense of numbers and develop flexibility in their number-sense reasoning.

When determining tools and technology to use in the unit, your team can clarify how certain tools are used to support or extend learning in the preK classroom. Discussions may focus on which tools are the most developmentally appropriate or contribute to other learning such as fine- and gross-motor skills too. It is important to note that any list of tools in preK is not an exhaustive list, but rather a sampling of key manipulatives that serve a specific instructional purpose.

Figure 3.10 (page 54) shows what teams could consider when selecting tools and technology so that all members of your preK team understand the purpose of each, its instructional implications, and how it might be used during assessments. (See figure 2.10, page 30, for the template with directions.)

Share as a team the managing of these materials within the classroom as well. How will students access these tools? Is there a routine in place for ensuring tools are used appropriately? Are there enough materials for the grade level? How will your preK team develop student self-efficacy in the choice and use of these tools for mathematical learning?

Your team has now thoughtfully considered each element of unit planning. This systematic process of unit planning would not be complete without embedding reflection into your team practices.

❼ Reflection and Notes

Team reflection occurs throughout the planning process as you remind each other of strategies to include and consider for the day-to-day details of lesson planning. These are the notes your team takes before and during the unit, as members plan together, creating an archive of their best ideas and approaches to learning.

Essential Learning Standard	Lower-Level Task Example	Higher-Level Task Example	School-Adopted Textbook Lessons	Explorations, Projects, or Activities	Supplemental or Online Resources
I can count from 1 to 10.	Choral counting during morning meeting	Start at 3, count on to 10.	PreK textbook chapter 1, lessons 3–5	Active counting such as with jumping jacks, toe touches, and knee lifts	Message in a Backpack™: Fun Ways to Build Your Child's Literacy Skills While Doing Laundry Together (Celano & Neuman, 2019; www.naeyc.org/resources/pubs/tyc/oct2019/backpack/build-literacy-doing-laundry) Print and send home to families.
I know numbers and can say the names.	Say the names of numerals in the correct sequence.	Recognize and say the names of numerals out of sequence.	PreK textbook chapter 1, lesson 6	Name and number sort	Illustrative Mathematics: www.illustrativemathematics.org • Task: Find the Numbers 0–5 or 5–10
I can count objects.	Count a set of (4) blocks.	Say, "Give me 8 blocks from this set."	PreK textbook chapter 1, lessons 7–9	Grab and count	Counting Collections: http://prek-math-te.stanford.edu/counting/counting-collections-overview
I can say how many I counted.	Ask, "How many did you just count?"	Cover set of objects and ask, "How many did you count?"	PreK textbook chapter 1, lessons 7–9	Hi Ho! Cherry-O	Classroom Videos: Counting (for team use during planning as a shared learning experience) • http://prek-math-te.stanford.edu/counting/classroom-videos-counting NCTM Illuminations: Okta's Rescue • www.nctm.org/Classroom-Resources/Illuminations/Interactives/Oktas-Rescue/ (For practice counting and subitizing)
I can say how many dots I see without counting.	Immediately state the number of dots arranged in a five frame.	Immediately state the number of dots arranged in a familiar pattern, like on a die.	PreK textbook chapter 3, Quick Image Routines	Games such as Candy Land, Chutes and Ladders, and so on, using dot dice	Illustrative Mathematics: www.illustrativemathematics.org • Task: Counting Mat NCTM Illuminations: Five Frame • www.nctm.org/Classroom-Resources/Illuminations/Interactives/Five-Frame/ (For practice counting and subitizing)
I can solve story problems.	I have 3 cookies. I ate one of them. How many cookies do I have left?	I have 5 crayons. Some are red and some are blue. How many red and blue crayons could I have?	PreK textbook chapter 3, lessons 1–5	Snack time problem solving Felt board stories during play	Team-developed problem types

Figure 3.9: Resources and activities for preK counting and cardinality unit.

Tool	Purpose	Instruction	Assessment
Counters (such as bears, blocks, beads, cubes, and so on)	Conceptual understanding Exploration	Count	Use during observations and interviews.
Linking cubes	Conceptual understanding Exploration	Count Join Separate	Use during observations and interviews.
Links	Conceptual understanding Exploration	Count Join Separate	Use during observations and interviews.
Dice or number cubes	Application Representations	Identify numerals Subitize	Use to generate random numbers to identify or dots to subitize during observations and interviews.
Number track My 1 to 10 Number Track 1 2 3 4 5 6 7 8 9 10	Conceptual understanding Exploration Application	Identify numerals Count Solve story problems	Make available during assessments as determined by the team.
Number cards	Conceptual understanding Application	Identify numerals Count Subitize Show representations	Use to generate random numbers during observations and interviews.
Dot cards	Application Representations	Subitize	Use during observations and interviews.
Rekenreks	Conceptual understanding Exploration	Count Join Separate	Use during observations and interviews.
Five and ten frames	Conceptual understanding Exploration Representations	Organize a set Subitize	Use during observations and interviews.

Technology	Purpose	Instruction	Assessment
Toy Theater virtual manipulatives: https://toytheater.com /category/teacher-tools /virtual-manipulatives/ (Two-color counters, five and ten frames, bear counters)	Exploration	Count Join Separate	Not applicable
Team-developed lessons using SMART Board	Exploration Representations	Count Join Separate	Not used on common assessments.

Figure 3.10: Tools and technology for preK counting and cardinality unit.

Equally important is the intentional reflection after the unit is complete. At the end of every unit, your preK team discusses student progress and considers making adjustments to the unit that are based on evidence of student learning resulting from your team practices throughout the unit.

Figure 3.11 (page 56) illustrates an example of team reflection and notes while planning the unit and after the unit of instruction. (See figure 2.11, page 31, for the template with directions.) Key considerations include listing the essential learning standards, making planning notes, and determining next steps.

The protocol in figure 3.11 (page 56) serves as an archive of your team successes, a living plan of next steps, and an honest dialogue about what is currently working or not working for your preK students. As you build trust among your team, consider the following guiding questions for supporting transparent and honest dialogue after your common assessments.

- Where in the data do you see a trend to celebrate?

- After looking at your classroom data, what questions would you like to ask your teammates?

- What would you like to know more about so that you can support each other in your mathematical teaching practices?

- Where in the data do you see evidence or need for adjusting your team's approach to teaching the standards in the unit?

Questions such as these encourage your team to openly reflect on your team's data and prepare you for moving forward instructionally. Through your team's reflection and routine sharing, you discover small, yet impactful, practices that help you reach more students.

Your preK team has now navigated through each element of a mathematics unit design. You started by identifying the essential learning standards and pacing the lessons and assessments using a unit calendar. Together, you have worked to agree on and clarify prior knowledge and vocabulary and notations. Your team also selected resources, tasks, tools, and technology to support lesson planning. You have included a process for recording notes when planning and for reflecting on the outcomes of the unit. Your team has now successfully generated the information needed to complete the Mathematics Unit Planner for your counting and cardinality unit.

PreK Counting and Cardinality Unit Planner

When your team thoughtfully plans a unit (like the counting and cardinality unit) before the unit begins, it strengthens your daily lesson design and team common assessments. Figure 3.12 (page 58) shows the completed Mathematics Unit Planner for this preK unit, capturing your team discussions and shared decisions. (See figure 1.2, page 11, for the template with directions.)

The counting and cardinality unit plan in figure 3.12 (page 58), with its accompanying calendar showing daily learning targets and common assessments (see figure 3.6, page 48), scores high on the Mathematics

Essential Learning Standard	Notes When Planning: What to Emphasize or Remember for Lessons and Assessments in the Unit	Team Reflections After the Unit
I can count from 1 to 10.	Ideas for supporting early counting: • Teacher recites short forward number sequences, and student copies or mimics • Teacher starts a counting sequence, and student says the next number • Student partners or teacher and student take turns participating in the counting sequence • Teacher intentionally makes a mistake in the counting sequence, and student corrects • Teacher asks the student to start the count from various places other than one	Our students who are only accurately reciting the counting sequence to 5 are going to get one-to-one re-engagement time with a teacher for ten minutes at least four days per week.
I know numbers and can say the names.	We want to use the name and number sort in this way: 1. Students sort letters in their name and numbers 0–9 to distinguish between letters and numbers. 2. Using their name tag for support, students spell their name to see the order of letters used to name things. 3. Using the number track, students match and order the numbers in the correct forward number sequence.	The numbers 6 and 9 seem to be giving our students the most trouble when identifying and naming numerals, which makes sense given how similar they are.
I can count objects.	Have these items available: • A variety of counting tools • Counting mats • Five and ten frames We are hoping to get outside to find counting collections in nature and encourage counting beyond the school walls. We will include pictures from these experiences in our newsletter to get families involved.	One of our teammates used a ten frame that was made from an egg carton to help students organize the count and start to subitize the amount in the frame. Another teammate used beads on a piece of yarn. Students could slide one bead at a time, and it significantly lowered the number of students who were double counting.
I can say how many I counted.	We are going to address cardinality and conservation (number of objects is the same if they are moved into a different arrangement) by doing the following during instruction and assessment: • After counting a set of objects, cover and ask, "How many did we just count?" • Then move the objects into a different arrangement and ask again, "How many do we have?"	We know some of our students just need more time with the concept of cardinality.

Essential Learning Standard	Notes When Planning: What to Emphasize or Remember for Lessons and Assessments in the Unit	Team Reflections After the Unit
I can say how many dots I see without counting.	Once we begin this instruction, we would like to include a daily routine and a plan to monitor what number quantities and images students are able to accurately and immediately identify.	Some of our students have been easily identifying single-dot images and five frames, so our plan to extend them includes: 1. Ten-frame images 2. Double-dot dice images with sums to ten
I can solve story problems.	We want to ensure this concept is taught not just using real-life contexts but also using relevant and in-the-moment contexts that are meaningful to our students. Example scenarios: • Giving a toy to a friend. • One student leaving the reading table. • Two kids are on the swings, and one more joins them. • Getting a snack from a friend or teacher.	Our students are most successful when we are adding on or taking away just one object.

Overall Unit Reflections: Things to Remember or Change for Next Year

While this is a unit of instruction with a start and end date, we just want to recognize that we are intentionally engaging our students in counting experiences throughout the year. We also have a wide range of learners, but this year we seem to have a larger number of students who are needing to be challenged or extended. We have specifically noted in our plans to extend learners in the following ways:

1. Rote counting to 20 and beyond (include use of a hundreds chart)
2. Counting backward
3. Naming the number after and before
4. Rote counting by fives and tens
5. Counting sets of objects beyond ten

Figure 3.11: Reflection and notes for preK counting and cardinality unit.

Unit: PreK Counting and Cardinality **Start Date:** March 2 **End Date:** April 3 **Total Number of Days:** 24	
Essential Learning Standards	• I can count from 1 to 10. • I know numbers and can say the names. • I can count objects. • I can say how many I counted. • I can say how many dots I see without counting. • I can solve story problems.
Prior Knowledge	**PreK (earlier in the year)** • Count from 1 to 5. • Recognize numerals to 5. • Count a set of 1 to 5 objects (one-to-one correspondence). • Count a set of 1 to 5 objects (cardinality). • Subitize 1 to 3 dots. • Join and separate up to 3 objects to model story problems.
Vocabulary and Notations	Numbers 0 through 10 (say the name of each) 0 through 10 (understand meaning of each) Count Notations (be able to identify): 0, 1, 2, 3, 4, 5, 6, 7, 8, 9, 10

Resources and Activities	• PreK texbook chapter 1, lessons 3–9
	• PreK textbook chapter 3, lessons 1–5
	• Active counting
	• Name and number sort
	• Grab and count
	• Hi Ho! Cherry-O
	• Board games with dot dice
	• Snack time problem solving
	• Felt board stories during play
	• Article for families: Message in a Backpack—Fun Ways to Build Your Child's Literacy Skills While Doing Laundry Together (www.naeyc.org/resources/pubs/tyc/oct2019/backpack/build-literacy-doing-laundry)
	• Illustrative Mathematics tasks: www.illustrativemathematics.org
	    ○ Find the Numbers 0–5 or 5–10
	    ○ Counting Mat
	• Counting Collections: http://prek-math-te.stanford.edu/counting/counting-collections-overview
	• Classroom Videos: Counting (http://prek-math-te.stanford.edu/counting/classroom-videos-counting)
	• Okta's Rescue: www.nctm.org/Classroom-Resources/Illuminations/Interactives/Oktas-Rescue
	• Five Frame: www.nctm.org/Classroom-Resources/Illuminations/Interactives/Five-Frame

Tools and Technology	• Counters (bears, blocks, beads, cubes, and so on) • Linking cubes • Links • Dice or number cubes • Number track • Number cards • Dot cards • Rekenreks • Five and ten frames • Toy Theater virtual manipulatives: https://toytheater.com/category/teacher-tools/virtual-manipulatives • Team-developed lessons using SMART Board
Reflection and Notes	When planning: Ideas for supporting early counting— • Teacher recites short forward number sequences, and student copies. • Teacher starts a counting sequence, and student says the next number. • Student partners or teacher and student take turns participating in the counting sequence. • Teacher intentionally makes a mistake in the counting sequence, and student corrects. • Teacher asks the student to start the count from various places other than one. We want to use the name and number sort in this way— • Students sort letters in their name and numbers 0–9 to distinguish between letters and numbers. • Using their name tag for support, students spell their name to see the order of letters used to name things. • Using the number track, match and order the numbers in the correct forward number sequence. Have these items available— • A variety of counting tools • Counting mats • Five and ten frames We are hoping to get outside to find counting collections in nature and encourage counting beyond the school walls. We will include pictures from these experiences in our newsletter to get families involved. We are going to address cardinality and conservation (number of objects is the same if they are moved into a different arrangement) by doing the following during instruction and assessment— • After counting a set of objects, cover and ask, "How many did we just count?" • Then move the objects into a different arrangement and ask again, "How many do we have?" Once we begin this instruction, we would like to include a daily routine and a plan to monitor what number quantities and images students are able to accurately and immediately identify. We want to ensure this concept is taught not just using real-life contexts but also using relevant and in-the-moment contexts that are meaningful to our students.

Figure 3.12: PreK counting and cardinality unit planner.

continued →

Reflection and Notes	Example scenarios—
	• Giving a toy to a friend
	• One student leaving the reading table
	• Two kids are on the swings, and one more joins them
	• Getting a snack from a friend or teacher
	After the unit:
	• Our students who are only accurately reciting the counting sequence to 5 are going to get one-to-one re-engagement time with a teacher for ten minutes at least four days per week.
	• The numbers 6 and 9 seem to be giving our students the most trouble when identifying and naming numerals, which makes sense given how similar they are.
	• One of our teammates used a ten frame that was made from an egg carton to help students organize the count and start to subitize the amount in the frame.
	• Another teammate used beads on a piece of yarn. Students could slide one bead at a time, and it significantly lowered the number of students who were double counting.
	• We know some of our students just need more time with the concept of cardinality.
	• Some of our students have been easily identifying single-dot images and five frames, so our plan to extend them includes:
	○ Ten-frame images
	○ Double-dot dice images with sums to ten
	• Our students are most successful when we are adding on or taking away just one object.
	Changes for next year:
	While this is a unit of instruction with a start and end date, we just want to recognize that we are intentionally engaging our students in counting experiences throughout the year. We also have a wide range of learners, but this year we seem to have a larger number of students who are needing to be challenged or extended. We have specifically noted in our plans to extend learners in the following ways—
	• Rote counting to 20 and beyond (include use of a hundreds chart)
	• Counting backward
	• Naming the number after and before
	• Rote counting by fives and tens
	• Counting sets of objects beyond ten

Unit Planning Rubric (figure 2.2, page 17). How will your team continue planning units for the year and document your discussions so your team can learn from these discussions from one unit to the next and one year to the next? How does each of your team's mathematics unit plans score against the rubric in figure 2.2 (page 17)? Your challenge as a team is to continue planning for each unit to strengthen both student and teacher learning.

Conclusion

Although this chapter discusses only one exemplar of a preK mathematics unit, each unit your team builds creates a foundational building block for your team to effectively ensure the learning of students across your grade-level team. Together, your clarity maximizes your instructional minutes and strengthens practices. Every member of your team and, more important, every student will benefit as you strive to achieve the self-efficacy promise that each and every student can learn the mathematics standards for preK.

The next chapter provides examples for the kindergarten *addition and subtraction to 10* unit plan. Whether the standards you see in the following unit plan are a direct match to your state standards or not, consider the key ideas your students will be expected to learn next year.

CHAPTER 4

Kindergarten Unit: Addition and Subtraction to 10

When students enter kindergarten, they bring their understanding of counting and cardinality and joining and separating from their learning in preK or other early-life experiences. In kindergarten, they grow this understanding. Through intentional unit design, your kindergarten team has an opportunity to build student confidence, self-efficacy, and a productive disposition with addition and subtraction to 10.

While many students who start kindergarten do so with backgrounds that include access to learning mathematics in a preK program the previous year, others do not. Students enter kindergarten with varied mathematical readiness and experiences. As your team plans your kindergarten units related to addition and subtraction to 10, start with clarity about what students should know and be able to do related to the learning arc for foundations of addition and subtraction in preK, first grade, and second grade. Keep in mind this will not be the first unit in a kindergartner's mathematics learning experience, but rather a culmination of understanding numbers to 10.

Students enrolled in a preK program learned to count to 10 and tell how many, subitize dots in arrangements up to 5, recognize and name numbers, and explore addition and subtraction within 5 by joining and separating objects when given a story problem. As first graders, your current kindergarten students will be expected to conceptually subitize (see images above 5 as two or more wholes) more than one image (for example, two ten frames or a domino), which leads to

second graders conceptually subitizing base-ten pieces. First graders will also fluently add and subtract within 10 while learning joining and separating strategies to add and subtract within 20, both with numbers in equations and when solving word problems with unknowns in various positions. In second grade, students will fluently add and subtract within 20 and learn to add and subtract within 100 (with special cases to 1,000), including solving both one- and two-step word problems.

When you have a clear understanding of the learning arc from grades preK–2, your team develops an understanding of the learning required in kindergarten mathematics. In kindergarten, counting objects expands from sets of ten or less in preK to sets of twenty or more. Students in kindergarten are also expected to apply counting skills to early arithmetic concepts such as interpreting joining and separating contexts or composing and decomposing 5 and 10 as well as teen numbers using a ten and ones.

Students at this early stage of making meaning with addition and subtraction are engaging in meaningful story problems that connect to their school experiences and daily life. Additionally, kindergarten students grow their ability to subitize objects and pictures by identifying quantities without counting, such as those they see on dot dice, organized on ten frames, and other structured arrangements. Subitizing plays a large role in developing number sense and understanding operations since it involves simultaneously recognizing a number as a whole set and as a sum of individual parts, especially when conceptually subitizing images larger than five.

The early counting and composing numbers experiences build the foundation for fluently adding and subtracting multidigit numbers. While students are expected to develop fluency with composing and decomposing numbers to 20 by second grade, much time is spent on building a conceptual understanding of addition and subtraction in the early primary grades to 10.

Trying to teach all addition and subtraction standards in one unit will most likely cause frustration; there are just so many concepts for students to learn. Therefore, your team most likely needs more than one addition and subtraction unit in kindergarten. Reference your district proficiency map or pacing guide to identify number and addition and subtraction units so your team has clarity about the specific state standards for addition and subtraction in each unit and how the standards might be spiraled or benchmarked over the course of the year.

The skills students learn in this sample unit could be a continuation of previously taught skills because children need plenty of experiences and practice over long periods of time to develop mastery.

This chapter focuses on sharing a mathematics unit example for how your kindergarten team might plan a unit using the essential standards related to *addition and subtraction to 10*. The standards that follow may or may not match your state standards, but most likely they contain the key ideas of some of your standards. These standards were first shared in table P2.1 (page 37) and are labeled *standards K.1–K.4*.

> **K.1. Use subitizing to instantly recognize a quantity of 1–10 using dot dice, five and ten frames, and other dot arrangements.**
>
> **K.2. Compose and decompose numbers less than or equal to 10 in more than one way using objects, drawings, fingers, and verbal expressions (for example, 5 is 3 and 2 or 4 and 1).**
>
> **K.3. Represent various verbal problem contexts involving joining and separating numbers to 10.**

> K.4. For any number from 1 to 9, find the number that makes 10 when added to the given number (for example, by using objects or drawings) and record the answer with a drawing or equation.

The bold standards reflect the need-to-know essential standards in the unit (see figure 2.3, page 19). These are the standards your team uses when creating common mid-unit assessments and uses first when addressing student learning gaps or extensions in learning. The more critical standards in the unit will be shared with you in either district documents or state, provincial, or national guidelines. They are not, however, the only standards students will learn in the unit. The standard not in bold is the important-to-know standard and will be taught by your team and included in your common end-of-unit assessment.

The distinction between these two sets of standards for this unit is that the bold standards incorporate prior learning experiences from preK or early-life experiences, and therefore, it is appropriate to expect a student in kindergarten to achieve mastery of these skills and concepts by the end of the year. Recognizing pairs of numbers that make sums of 10 is new, and during first grade, students will engage in ample opportunities to sharpen their skills and develop fluency with sums to 10.

Since the three bold standards represent the big ideas students need as they leave kindergarten, students will use tools to build an understanding of composing and decomposing 5 and 10. They will use this knowledge as they begin to develop fact fluency in first grade. Kindergarten students are asked to think flexibly to show different number combinations, which leads to further problem solving in first and second grade.

Once your team has clarity about the standards in the unit and how they fit in the foundations of the addition and subtraction story arc of a kindergartener, it is time for you to begin creating your unit plan. The Mathematics Unit Planner will guide your team and provide a location to record your agreements (see figure 1.2, page 11). Your team's work starts with generating essential learning standards in student-friendly language for assessment and reflection.

❶ Essential Learning Standards

Now that your kindergarten team has clarified the need-to-know and important-to-know standards in the addition and subtraction to 10 unit, you can determine the essential learning standards. The essential learning standards are the driver for your common assessments and student reflections related to learning. They are written as *I can* statements and generated from the state standards students must learn in the unit and form the daily learning targets for lessons.

So, what *exactly* do students have to know and be able to do? Together, use the team protocol to unwrap and make sense of mathematics standards to answer this critical question as shown in figure 2.4 (page 20). Examples of completed templates for the need-to-know standards of the unit are shown in figures 4.1 (page 64), 4.2 (page 65), and 4.3 (page 66).

Unwrapping standard K.1 in figure 4.1 (page 64) will help each teacher on your team deepen his or her understanding of early addition and subtraction and the need for subitizing. Your team will also clarify the depth of understanding students must have to be proficient. Team members may share different instructional strategies to use when teaching students to compose and decompose numbers so students can *see* numbers (use arrangements of dots or manipulatives without having to count each). Record these strategies in the last part of the Mathematics Unit Planner under Reflection and Notes (see figure 1.2, page 11).

Your team may decide to include visuals that represent a variety of dot images in your student-friendly essential learning standard ("I can say how many dots I see") since these are examples of arrangements of what students might see. Students have an easier time subitizing rectangular arrangements, small quantities in a line, or dot images that involve symmetry. Thinking ahead with your team about the structured images you will use enhances number routines and lessons.

Standard K.2 in figure 4.2 (page 65) relates to standard K.1 (see figure 4.1, page 64) since the visualizing of dot patterns supports students developing an understanding of addition combinations and the early development of fact fluency.

As your team makes sense of standard K.2, you might discuss the difference between tools students use to develop understanding and the counting strategies that students employ to determine combinations. For example, tools for developing understanding might include using two-colored discs or linking cubes to represent addition and subtraction. A kindergartener might use strategies such as to begin with counting all or each within a set and later become more efficient by counting on from the larger number.

During the process of unwrapping standards like those shown in figure 4.1 (page 64) and figure 4.2 (page 65), your team can discuss how students are expected to show proficiency with each standard on your common end-of-unit assessment or your common ongoing assessment given at multiple checkpoints during the year. A clear picture of the end goal can support your grade-level team as it generates ideas and navigates conversations that lead to being ready to complete the components of the unwrapping protocol, especially those related to tasks and student proficiency levels.

Standards sometimes include very formal jargon, which can lead you and your teammates to varied interpretations. The process of circling verbs and underlining noun phrases is meant to bring a clarity and focus to what students must know and be able to do. Clarity comes from the meaningful conversations you have as a team during the process.

There is a clear connection between the composing and decomposing of numbers in standard K.2 (figure 4.2, page 65) and the story problems that students interpret in standard K.3 (figure 4.3, page 66). Therefore, it is important to note that these standards are not meant to be taught separately, one before the other; rather, the ability to break numbers apart and put numbers together relies on the sense making that occurs when dealing with a real-life context. For example, when finding a missing addend, some students will see a problem as an *adding on* situation and others will *take away* to find the missing value.

Unit: Kindergarten—Addition and Subtraction to 10	
State Standard in the Unit:	
K.1. Use subitizing to instantly recognize a quantity of 1–10 using dot dice, five and ten frames, and other dot arrangements.	
Conceptual Understanding **What do students need to know?**	**Procedural Knowledge and Skills** **What do students need to do?**
<ul><li>1–10 as quantities</li><li>Dot dice images 1–10</li><li>Five-frame images</li><li>Ten-frame images</li><li>Other dot arrangements 1–10</li></ul>	<ul><li>Subitize (instantly recognize) small sets of dot images 1–10.</li><li>Recognize a small quantity of arranged images without having to count each one 1–10.</li><li>Explain how to see groups of dots when subitizing.</li></ul>

Academic Vocabulary and Notations				
Numbers	Count	Dot images	Five frame	Ten frame

Essential Learning Standard

(In student-friendly language—I can . . .)

- I can quickly say how many dots I see.

Proficiency Level of Understanding	
4 **Advanced**	Instantly recognize dot images 1–10 or larger arranged in familiar and in less structured patterns.
3 **Proficient**	Instantly recognize dot images 1–10 arranged in familiar patterns such as dot dice and five- and ten-frame images.
2 **Partial**	Instantly recognize single-dot images 1–5 arranged in familiar patterns such as dot dice and five-frame images.
1 **Minimal**	Instantly recognize only single-dot images with small quantities 1–3 and primarily count dots in images.

Exemplar Tasks to Meet Standard:

Task 1—Same, More, Less

A student or student pairs select a starting card. Using various other dot cards, students determine whether the value is the same, more, or less than the starting card.

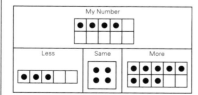

Task 2—Sorting Values

Students use a mat to sort values of various dot images. Ranges of number values can be changed to best fit the needs of students.

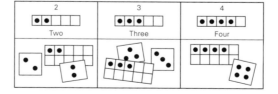

Task 3—Image and Finger Flash Routine

The teacher flashes a dot image (quickly so students cannot count the dots) and then covers it. Students can respond orally or students show the value being displayed with their fingers. The teacher can expand on the idea by asking students to show the value in more than one way. Ask, "Show me with your fingers how many dots you see. Can you make this number with your fingers a different way?"

Figure 4.1: Unwrap and make sense of standard K.1.

Unit: Kindergarten—Addition and Subtraction to 10

State Standard in the Unit:

K.2. Compose and decompose numbers less than or equal to 10 in more than one way using objects, drawings, fingers, and verbal expressions (for example, 5 is 3 and 2 or 4 and 1).

Conceptual Understanding What do students need to know?	Procedural Knowledge and Skills What do students need to do?

• Numbers less than or equal to 10
• Combinations of numbers to 10 or less
• Representations of combinations of numbers using
  ○ Objects
  ○ Drawings
  ○ Fingers
  ○ Verbal expressions
	• Compose and decompose 10 and numbers less than 10 in various ways.
	• Express combinations of numbers within 10 orally.
	• Use objects, drawings, and fingers to show the part-part-whole relationship when composing and decomposing numbers within 10.
	• Add or put numbers together within 10.
	• Subtract or take numbers apart from numbers as large as 10.

Academic Vocabulary and Notations
Compose   Add (+)   Subtract (−)   Equals (=)

Essential Learning Standard (In student-friendly language—I can . . .)
• I can make and break apart numbers to 10.

Proficiency Level of Understanding	
4 **Advanced**	Compose and decompose numbers to 10 and greater using flexible number and counting strategies such as counting the imagined or counting on.
3 **Proficient**	Compose and decompose numbers less than or equal to 10 by modeling with objects, drawings, fingers, and verbally.
2 **Partial**	Compose and decompose numbers less than or equal to 5 by modeling with objects, drawings, fingers, and verbally.
1 **Minimal**	With support, compose and decompose numbers less than or equal to 5 by modeling with objects, drawings, and fingers.

Exemplar Tasks to Meet Standard:

Task 1—Bowl of Fruit

Trent has 10 pieces of fruit in his bowl. Some are apples and some are bananas.

How many apples and how many bananas could Trent have?

Example response:

"Four apples and six bananas are 10 fruits in all."

Task 2: Towers—Adding One, Two, or Three

Roll a dot cube to determine how tall the tower will be. Spin the spinner to determine how many to add on. Say or record how many altogether.

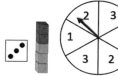

Task 3:

Show two different ways to make 7.

(Students may show their answer using two groups of objects or by writing equations.)

Figure 4.2: Unwrap and make sense of standard K.2.

Unit: Kindergarten—Addition and Subtraction to 10

State Standard in the Unit:

K.3. (Represent) various verbal problem contexts involving (joining) and (separating) numbers to 10.

Conceptual Understanding What do students need to know?	Procedural Knowledge and Skills What do students need to do?
• Representations within 10 using objects and pictures • Verbal context problems with numbers to 10	• Represent various verbal story contexts to show joining and separating within 10 with a focus on the unknown as the result. • Use concrete objects, pictorial models, verbal expressions, and flexible number strategies to represent the operations during problem solving.

Academic Vocabulary and Notations

Story problem

Essential Learning Standard (In student-friendly language—I can . . .)

• I can solve story problems.

Proficiency Level of Understanding	
4 Advanced	Represent joining and separating contexts, with numbers up to or beyond 10, with the unknown in different positions (for example, $3 + ? = 12$, $15 - ? = 10$, $7 + 4 = ?$, or $? + 3 = 8$).
3 Proficient	Represent joining and separating contexts with numbers up to 10, where the result is unknown and part-part-whole problem contexts where the whole is unknown (for example, $3 + 5 = ?$ or $7 - 6 = ?$).
2 Partial	Represent joining and separating contexts where the result is unknown and part-part-whole problem contexts where the whole is unknown with numbers up to 5.
1 Minimal	With support, represent joining and separating contexts where the result is unknown and part-part-whole problem contexts where the whole is unknown with numbers up to 5.

Exemplar Task to Meet Standard:

Task 1—Playground Tasks

a. There are 3 children at the playground. 4 more children come to play.
    How many children are at the playground?

b. There are 6 children at the playground. 2 children leave to go home.
    How many children are at the playground now?

c. There are 3 boys and 5 girls at the playground.
    How many children are there in all at the playground?

Figure 4.3: Unwrap and make sense of standard K.3.

Once your team has similarly made sense of the remaining important-to-know standard, you can combine the information to generate the unit essential learning standards and daily learning targets from your unwrapped standards (see figure 4.4, page 68). (See figure 2.5, page 22, for the template with directions.)

Your kindergarten team can put the information in the center column of figure 4.4 (page 68) into the first row of the Mathematics Unit Planner for the kindergarten addition and subtraction to 10 unit (see figure 4.11, page 79).

Sometimes teams group together state standards that closely align to form one student-friendly essential learning standard; however, grouping standards is not needed in this unit because each essential learning standard can be assessed separately with meaningful student reflection for each one. Additionally, there are only four essential learning standards in the unit, which falls within the targeted range of three to six standards per unit. The daily learning targets are from the concepts and skills portion of the unwrapping work and share the story of learning in the unit.

Both the essential learning standards and daily learning targets provide resources for your team as you plan your lessons and assessments. The next step for team unit planning is to add the dates for common assessments to the calendar and create the learning story arc with the daily learning targets.

❷ Unit Calendar

The unit calendar includes common assessment dates and student-friendly targets that help shape the story of learning about to take place. The unit calendar is not meant to be a lockstep approach to teaching among team members. Rather, the goal is to have an agreed-on time expectation to spend on each essential learning standard by following the general order of learning targets to be addressed.

Gathering formative evidence of student learning will happen in an ongoing way throughout the addition and subtraction to 10 unit. Your kindergarten team will use the three bold standards in the unit to develop your mid-unit common checklists and assessment tasks.

The process of assessing young learners can be time consuming since it involves observing students' strategies and listening to their oral explanations. Consider when and how frequently assessments should occur during the unit (preferably after appropriate amounts of exploration and practice has happened) for the most meaningful student and teacher reflection. Consider, too, when the unit must end and how many days to allocate to instruction and assessment. The common end-of-unit assessment will include all four of the essential learning standards in the unit. Also, are there any holidays or non-teaching days to note and plan around? Should there be flex days scheduled for teachers to respond to student needs based on the formative data they have collected?

One possible way for your kindergarten team to plan for student learning and common assessments in the addition and subtraction to 10 unit appears in the calendar in figure 4.5 (page 69). (See figure 2.6, page 24, for the template with directions.) This is not the first time that students will work with subitizing, adding, or subtracting. They have done work with these concepts and skills in earlier units to 5 and through number routines to 10 during the year.

If this is the first time your team is making the calendar, start with identifying the dates of your agreed-on common assessments in the unit. Next, work together as a team to plan the flow of the unit, but understand that through the reflection during each unit, the flow and storyline will become stronger and more precise each year.

Should your team decide ending dates need to change during a unit, it is important to communicate possible changes with one another. Consult your proficiency map or yearlong pacing guide to make sure you still have time for the remaining mathematics units. Record any changes in the Reflection and Notes portion of the Mathematics Unit Planner (see figure 1.2, page 11) to remember them for the next year.

Once your team has an agreed-on calendar and storyline for the unit, the next step is to discuss the prior knowledge students are expected to be proficient with before the unit of instruction begins.

Formal Unit Standards (State Standard Language)	Essential Learning Standards for Assessment and Reflection (Student-Friendly Language)	Daily Learning Targets What students must know and be able to do for each lesson (unwrapped standards) (Storyboard Progression)
K.1. Use subitizing to instantly recognize a quantity of 1–10 using dot dice, five and ten frames, and other dot arrangements.	• I can quickly say how many dots I see.	Students will be able to: • Subitize (instantly recognize) small sets of dot images 1–10 • Recognize a small quantity of arranged images without having to count each one 1–10 • Tell how to see the dots when dot image groups contain more than 5 (conceptual subitizing)
K.2. Compose and decompose numbers less than or equal to 10 in more than one way using objects, drawings, fingers, and verbal expressions (for example, 5 is 3 and 2 or 4 and 1).	• I can make and break apart numbers to 10.	Students will be able to: • Compose and decompose 10 and numbers less than 10 in various ways • Express combinations within 10 orally • Use objects, drawings, and fingers to compose and decompose numbers within 10 • Add or put numbers together within 10 • Subtract or take numbers apart within 10
K.3. Represent various verbal problem contexts involving joining and separating numbers to 10.	• I can solve story problems.	Students will be able to: • Represent various verbal story contexts to show joining and separating within 10 • Use concrete objects, pictorial models, verbal expressions, and flexible number strategies to represent the operations during problem solving
K.4. For any number from 1 to 9, find the number that makes 10 when added to the given number (for example, by using objects or drawings) and record the answer with a drawing or equation.	• I can show ways to make 10.	Students will be able to: • Show how to make a 10, given a number from 1 to 9, using objects, drawings, or flexible number strategies • Find the number that makes 10, given a number from 1 to 9, and record the answers using drawings or equations

Figure 4.4: Kindergarten addition and subtraction to 10 unit standards, essential learning standards, and daily learning targets.

Monday	Tuesday	Wednesday	Thursday	Friday
2/23 Teacher workday	2/24 Count and subitize dot images	2/25 Count and subitize dot images	2/26 Count and subitize dot images	2/27 Count and subitize dot images
3/2 **Common Mid-Unit Assessment:** • I can quickly say how many dots I see.	3/3 **Common Mid-Unit Assessment:** • I can quickly say how many dots I see.	3/4 Subitize dot images and solve story problems for joining	3/5 Subitize dot images and solve story problems for joining	3/6 Subitize dot images and solve story problems for joining
3/9 Subitize dot images and solve story problems for joining and separating	3/10 Subitize dot images and solve story problems for joining and separating	3/11 Compose and decompose numbers within 10 using story problems	3/12 Compose and decompose numbers within 10 Students make story problems	3/13 Compose and decompose numbers within 10 Students make story problems
3/16 **Common Mid-Unit Assessment:** • I can make and break apart numbers to 10. • I can solve story problems.	3/17 **Common Mid-Unit Assessment:** • I can make and break apart numbers to 10. • I can solve story problems.	3/18 Make a 10 given a number in a story problem context	3/19 Subitize and make a 10 given a number	3/20 Subitize and make a 10 given a number
3/23 Flex day to respond to student needs	3/24 Flex day to respond to student needs	3/25 **Common End-of-Unit Assessment:** • I can quickly say how many dots I see. • I can make and break apart numbers to 10. • I can solve story problems. • I can show ways to make 10.	3/26 **Common End-of-Unit Assessment:** • I can quickly say how many dots I see. • I can make and break apart numbers to 10. • I can solve story problems. • I can show ways to make 10.	3/27 **Common End-of-Unit Assessment:** • I can quickly say how many dots I see. • I can make and break apart numbers to 10. • I can solve story problems. • I can show ways to make 10.

Figure 4.5: Kindergarten addition and subtraction to 10 unit calendar.

❸ Prior Knowledge

Before you and your team begin to plan lessons or choose mathematical tasks, it is important to determine the prerequisite content knowledge students need in order to access the kindergarten content in the current unit. Before this unit, students have been learning to count, write numbers, subitize, and compose and decompose numbers within 5. They may have even explored numbers to 10 and teen numbers.

Figure 4.6 is an example of a protocol that identifies the skills and prior-knowledge standards from earlier units taught in kindergarten or from standards learned in preK. (See figure 2.7, page 25, for the template with directions.) Once your team identifies the prior-knowledge standards, the protocol asks that you summarize the standard so it is student friendly in the Mathematics Unit Planner (see figure 1.2, page 11). The last column in figure 4.6 matches the prior knowledge in the kindergarten addition and subtraction to 10 unit planner (see figure 4.11, page 79).

Start your lessons by using tasks and activities that connect to the day's learning target and prior knowledge skills as Kanold, Kanold-McIntyre, et al. (2018) discuss in *Mathematics Instruction and Tasks in a PLC at Work.* (Visit **go.SolutionTree.com/MathematicsatWork** for free reproducibles.) In the addition and subtraction to 10 unit, mastery of one-to-one counting is important prior knowledge. You can embed routines for developing number sense using ten-frame number talks as lesson openers to provide an opportunity for students to explore number combinations.

After you and your team identity the prior knowledge for the unit, the next task is to determine the mathematics vocabulary and notations that students need to learn and use throughout the unit.

❹ Vocabulary and Notations

One of the mathematics process standards calls for students to use appropriate academic language when discussing mathematics. For you to support students' use of the academic language, you and your team will need to identify the mathematics vocabulary words, visuals that support learning the language, and any notations (symbols) students will need to precisely use, read, write, and speak to clearly communicate. Consider how students will learn the vocabulary and notations in real time through strong lesson design.

When unwrapping standards, your team identifies mathematics vocabulary words such as *count*, *add*, and *subtract* and number names that students will need to understand and use to fully learn the essential learning standards in the unit.

Figure 4.7 (page 72) shows a completed sample protocol that includes visual vocabulary displays your team might consider for creating a word wall or anchor chart as kindergarteners learn the words and notations in the addition and subtraction to 10 unit. (See figure 2.8, page 27, for the template and directions.) List the words and notations in the addition and subtraction to 10 mathematics unit planner (see figure 4.11, page 79).

The examples in figure 4.7 (page 72) show that students use drawings to record the mathematics they are learning. In kindergarten, the emphasis on recording work using equations occurs later in the year after students have practiced writing numerals and using objects and pictures to understand addition and subtraction. In this unit, students share thinking through modeling with tools and explaining ideas verbally. They begin to record their work using pictures and, later, expressions (for example, 3 + 4) and equations (for example, 3 + 4 = 7). Proficiency with concepts, however, may not require accurate written equations. A teacher may note student strategies and ideas on anchor charts, take and share pictures of representations created with physical models, and provide sentence stems to support oral communication. This development of pictorial representations is further emphasized in first grade while students continue to learn how to record their thinking using equations.

In *Mathematics Instruction and Tasks in a PLC at Work* (Kanold, Kanold-McIntyre, et al., 2018), there are several ideas for how to infuse the learning of vocabulary and notations into daily lessons as a component of quality lesson design. (Visit **go.SolutionTree.com/ MathematicsatWork** for free reproducibles.) Keep in mind, your team will find it helpful to connect with the preK, first-, and second-grade teams to align vocabulary and notations to grow student learning.

Formal Unit Standards (State Standard Language)	Essential Learning Standards for Assessment and Reflection (Student-Friendly Language)	Prior-Knowledge Standards From Prior Grade Level, Course, or Unit	Prior-Knowledge Summary With Exemplars
K.1. Use subitizing to instantly recognize a quantity of 1–10 using dot dice, five and ten frames, and other dot arrangements.	• I can quickly say how many dots I see.	**PreK:** Subitize single images 1–5 including dot dice, five frames, and other dot arrangements.	• Subitize images showing 1–5. Which show only 2?
K.2. Compose and decompose numbers less than or equal to 10 in more than one way using objects, drawings, fingers, and verbal expressions (for example, 5 is 3 and 2 or 4 and 1).	• I can make and break apart numbers to 10.	**PreK and kindergarten:** Count a set of 1–10 objects with one count per object. Understand that the last count indicates how many objects were counted.	• Count a set of 1–10 objects. Give me 5 blocks. How many blocks did you just give me?
K.3. Represent various verbal problem contexts involving joining and separating numbers to 10.	• I can solve story problems.	**PreK and kindergarten:** Use concrete objects, pictorial models, and verbal problem contexts for joining and separating up to 5 objects.	• Join and separate up to 5. Mike has 3 cookies in his snack box. Mary gives him 1 more cookie. How many cookies does Mike have?
K.4. For any number from 1 to 9, find the number that makes 10 when added to the given number (for example, by using objects or drawings) and record the answer with a drawing or equation.	• I can show ways to make 10.	**PreK and kindergarten:** Use concrete objects, pictorial models, and verbal problem contexts to combine numbers to make 5.	• Explore different ways to combine numbers to make 5. I have 5 apples. Some are red and some are green. How many red and green apples can I have?

Figure 4.6: Prior-knowledge standards for kindergarten addition and subtraction to 10 unit.

Unit: Kindergarten—Addition and Subtraction to 10	
Vocabulary	**Definition, Explanation, Drawing, or Example**
Zero through ten (Identify the numerals, and hear and say the name for each number from 0 to 10)	0 zero — 1 • one — 2 •• Two — 3 ••• Three — ... — 10 •••• •••• •• Ten
Dot images, five and ten frames	Dot Images Five Frame Ten Frame
Add	To join or put together **Add** Join together ◼◼◼◼◼ "2 and 3 is 5 altogether."
Subtract	To take away from, take apart, or compare **Subtract** Take apart ◼◼◼ ◼ "If I take 1 away from 4, I will still have 3 left."
Story problem	Math question that includes words and numbers **Story Problem** 3 birds were on a branch. 1 bird flew away. How many birds are left?

Notation	Words to Show How to Read the Notation	Example Showing How to Use the Notation in a Mathematics Expression or Equation
+	Plus or add	$9 + 1$
−	Minus, take away, or subtract	$8 - 6$
=	Is the same as (or equals)	$5 + 1 = 6$
Pictures to represent joining	Three children and two more children make five altogether	
Pictures to represent separating	Four take away one is three	

Figure 4.7: Vocabulary and notations protocol for kindergarten addition and subtraction to 10 unit.

The center of student learning during a mathematics lesson occurs through your team's choice of mathematics tasks and the student reasoning required to complete each task. The next part of the Mathematics Unit Planner (see figure 1.2, page 11) asks you and your collaborative team to identify the tasks, portions of lessons in curriculum materials, and supplemental resources and activities needed for students to learn the standards in the unit.

❺ Resources and Activities

Composing and decomposing numbers in different ways is the foundation of adding and subtracting. What are the best types of tasks to develop both conceptual understanding of joining and separating while beginning to develop procedural fluency with addition and subtraction? Your kindergarten collaborative team identifies any common resources or activities that will effectively help every student learn the grade-level essential learning standards.

Once your team has clarity on the essential learning standards and examples of mathematical tasks to use for instruction and assessment, it is time to consider your resources. Your team should consider the following questions.

- Which parts of our school-adopted textbooks or program correlate to the standards in the unit?

- Which are the best lessons or tasks to use in our books or program?

- Are there lessons or tasks to omit in a chapter or program because they don't match the standards in the unit?

- What ongoing centers or learning stations should we prepare to include?

- Is there a need for additional explorations, activities, or lessons because our book or program does not fully teach each essential learning standard? If so, what other resources should we use or develop?

Figure 4.8 (page 74) shows possible answers to the preceding questions plus examples of lower- and higher-level-cognitive-demand tasks for the essential learning standards in the unit. (See figure 2.9, page 28, for the template with directions.) Some parts of the chart are blank because, for example, your kindergarten team may decide that the lessons in the textbook

Essential Learning Standard	Lower-Level Task Example	Higher-Level Task Example	School-Adopted Textbook Lessons	Explorations, Projects, or Activities	Supplemental or Online Resources
I can quickly say how many dots I see.	How many dots do you see? How do you know?	How many dots do you see? How do you know?		Sorting station Mix and mingle: Find a partner with the same amount	Team-developed subitizing dot cards and finger flash cards
I can make and break apart numbers to 10.	I have 3 red blocks and 4 blue blocks. How many blocks do I have in all?	I have 7 blocks altogether. I can see 3 of them. The rest are hidden under the mat. How many blocks are under the mat? How do you know? Mat	Book 6, Lessons 1.1–1.4	One more, one less station	Virginia Department of Education: www.doe.virginia.gov/testing/sol/standards_docs/mathematics/2016/mip/index.shtml Task: Bears in Caves
I can solve story problems.	I have 6 bananas. If I eat two of them, how many do I still have?	I have 6 bananas. I eat some of them. Now I have 4 bananas. How many bananas did I eat?	Book 6, Lessons 2.1–2.6	Create your own story problem with scenario mats	Team-developed act-it-out problem solving
I can show ways to make 10.	How many more do you need to make ten? (Show students 6 cubes.)	Show as many ways to make ten using objects, pictures, numbers, or words. How will you know if you have all the ways?	Book 6, Lessons 2.7–2.8	Compatible numbers Ten-frame puzzles	Illustrative Mathematics: www.illustrativemathematics.org Task: Ten Frame Addition

Figure 4.8: Resources and activities for kindergarten addition and subtraction to 10 unit.

series or program aren't as effective as the supplemental or online resources. In other units, your team might determine your textbook or program is strong and no supplemental resources are needed.

Your kindergarten team should select a balance of higher- and lower-level-cognitive-demand tasks that match the rigor that proficient students demonstrate. Through this practice, you are contributing to a shared bank of resources. It is here—in the selection of resources—that the most significant teacher learning may occur as your team archives what to use for instruction from year to year. Your resources are intentionally kept, adjusted, or discarded based on your team's evidence of student learning.

After your team plans the learning experiences and determines any common resources and activities to use in the unit, add the information in the Mathematics Unit Planner (see figure 4.11, page 79). Now your team has just one more element of the unit planner to agree on—the technology and tools students should use during instruction and assessment.

❻ Tools and Technology

When planning for a unit on addition and subtraction to 10, which tools or manipulatives do students need for meaningful explorations leading to conceptual understanding? How can tools or technology support extending deeper student understanding of composing and decomposing numbers?

Together, your team members determine the tools and technology students should use for learning purposes. Tools are instruments used to employ a variety of strategies while learning or demonstrating learning, and, in kindergarten, tools are often the concrete objects and manipulatives students use to develop meaning of the content they are learning. Be sure to discuss which technology and tools students can use on common assessments and when students might need to minimize their use of the tool during instruction, if at all. It might be tempting to discuss strategies too, or to reflect as a team on how the same tool might be used to employ different strategies. While the following example protocol shows which tools your team might use during the unit, teaching strategies can be documented in the Reflection and Notes section of the Mathematics Unit Planner (see figure 1.2, page 11).

Figure 4.9 (page 76) shows an example of tools and technology your team could agree to use in the unit and the purpose of each. In kindergarten, tools are generally used for both instruction and assessment, which you will see noted in the template. (See figure 2.10, page 30, for the template with directions.) Consider how your team can use each tool to develop conceptual understanding for students as they learn strategies for addition and subtraction and then grow these strategies to using pictures, and finally, to using numbers and equations to show addition and subtraction reasoning. Then, add the information to the Tools and Technology section in the Mathematics Unit Planner (see figure 4.11, page 79).

Students in the early primary grades need many experiences with concrete materials in order to build an understanding of concepts. This means your kindergarten team might need to consider how teachers will manage tools in the classroom and determine how students will access tools during whole-group and small-group instruction, and during independent practice. Explicit teaching and modeling may be necessary for students to effectively use tools or technology.

Your team has thoughtfully answered PLC at Work critical question 1, *What do we want all students to know and be able to do?* related to addition and subtraction to 10. For the unit, you have worked together to clearly articulate the standards, choose tasks, and select appropriate tools. The final part of the Mathematics Unit Planner (see figure 1.2, page 11) provides space to record reflection and notes for future reference, either while teaching the unit or after it ends.

❼ Reflection and Notes

Your kindergarten team most likely engaged in many rich and meaningful conversations that included determining mathematical strategies to use when supporting student learning as you planned your unit. You continue your team conversations related to practices and strategies after each common mid-unit assessment as you determine the instructional strategies that are working or not working. And, when the unit ends, your team reflects on the practices and strategies to use in the future and which, if any, to discard. Where does your team keep the historical knowledge of the unit? The systematic process of unit design would not be complete without including a protocol for Reflection and Notes.

Tool	Purpose	Instruction	Assessment
Counters (bears, blocks, two-colored counters, and so on)	Conceptual understanding Exploration	Counting	Use during observations and interviews.
Linking cubes	Conceptual understanding Exploration	Counting Joining Separating	Use during observations and interviews.
Rekenreks	Conceptual understanding Exploration	Counting Joining Separating	Use during observations and interviews.
Five and ten frames	Conceptual understanding Exploration Representations	Organize a set of objects Subitize	Use during observations and interviews.
Part-part-whole mats	Conceptual understanding Exploration Representations Application	Organize a set of objects Subitize	Use during observations and interviews.
Number line	Conceptual understanding Exploration Justification	Add and subtract	Use as needed by the student.
Dot cards	Application Representations	Subitize Share how to group dots	Use during observations and interviews.
Dominoes	Application Representation	Subitize Share how to group dots	Use during observations and interviews.
Dice or number cubes	Exploration Application	Subitize Generate addition or subtraction expressions	Use during observations and interviews.

Technology	Purpose	Instruction	Assessment
Toy Theater virtual manipulatives: https://toytheater.com/category/teacher-tools/virtual-manipulatives/ (Two-color counters, five and ten frames, bear counters)	Exploration	Counting Joining Separating	Not used on common assessments.
NCTM Illuminations Ten Frame https://www.nctm.org/Classroom-Resources/Illuminations/Interactives/Ten-Frame/	Exploration Representations	Counting Subitizing Problem solving	Not used on common assessments.
Team-developed lessons using SMART Board	Exploration Representations	Counting Joining Separating Subitizing Problem solving	Not used on common assessments.

Figure 4.9: Tools and technology for kindergarten addition and subtraction to 10 unit.

Figure 4.10 (page 78) shows an example of team reflection and notes on the kindergarten addition and subtraction to 10 unit. (See figure 2.11, page 31, for the template with directions.)

The protocol in figure 4.10 (page 78) serves as an archive of your team successes, a living plan of next steps, and a conversation about what is currently working or not working for your kindergarten learners. As you build trust among your team, consider the following guiding questions for supporting transparent and honest dialogue after your common end-of-unit assessment.

- Where in the data do you see a trend to celebrate?

- After looking at your classroom data, what questions would you like to ask your teammates?

- What would you like to know more about to support one another's mathematical teaching practices?

- Where in the data do you see evidence of a need to adjust your team's approach to teaching the standards in the unit?

Questions such as these encourage members to openly reflect about data and prepare them for moving forward instructionally.

Your kindergarten team has identified the essential learning standards from the state standards in the kindergarten addition and subtraction to 10 unit. Together, your team worked to agree on and clarify the prior knowledge, vocabulary and notations, resources and activities, and tools and technology. Along the way and after the unit ended, your team recorded reflections and notes. Your team has now successfully generated the information needed to complete the Mathematics Unit Planner for your foundations of addition and subtraction unit.

Kindergarten Addition and Subtraction to 10 Unit Planner

When your team plans a unit (like the addition and subtraction to 10 unit) before the unit begins, it strengthens daily lesson design and team common assessments. Figure 4.11 (page 79) shows the completed Mathematics Unit Planner for the kindergarten addition and subtraction to 10 unit, summarizing your

Essential Learning Standard	Notes When Planning: What to Emphasize or Remember for Lessons and Assessments in the Unit	Team Reflections After the Unit
I can quickly say how many dots I see.	Continue using our daily routine that we developed in the early fall and stations that allow for continued student practice independently or with teacher guidance.	Since we now have a spreadsheet checklist to monitor subitizing, we were able to see quickly who was proficient, close to proficient, and far from proficient. We have several students ready for subitizing double images and more complex patterns and can determine at the next assessment window if they will be beyond proficient. We will reassess in three weeks after continued guided instruction and practice.
I can make and break apart numbers to 10.	We want to make sure to emphasize the language of joining and separating rather than focusing on the symbolic use of the plus, minus, and equal signs. Examples: • 2 and 6 is the same as 5 and 3 • 6 take away 1 is 5	Our students who are still inconsistently counting one-to-one need the most extra time and support. We are putting all five students into one group. During math workshop, they will re-engage in counting, joining, and separating lessons three times per week for 12 to 15 minutes each lesson.
I can solve story problems.	Last year we had a lot of success using the act-it-out kits and story mats. Students solved given problems and created their own. We want to do this again and need time for students to create their own.	Many students can solve problems in a variety of joining and separating contexts, but we are noticing that an area of weakness is recording their thinking. We are thinking about experimenting with this plan moving forward: • Use iPads to record videos of students solving problems using tools, and share the videos during guided instruction. • Have the teacher scribe what the student is saying or doing using words, pictures, and/or numbers. • Transition to the students representing thinking with words, pictures, or numbers to describe how they solved the problems.
I can show ways to make 10.	Using ten frames and our fingers are critical for developing the concept of 10. So, we need to make sure to intentionally plan for opportunities to utilize these tools. It will be important to observe who can subitize the frames and their own fingers rather than always having to rely on counting all or from 1.	Our results using the team-developed observation tool: **Making Tens Assessment** | Strategy Used	Percent of Students
---	---
Immediate recall of tens	17%
Subitized an image or fingers	36%
Counting on from the larger number	20%
Counts all and starts at 1	18%
No access	9%	 We were so excited to see the number of students who were not having to rely on a counting-all strategy. It seems that our combination of subitizing routine and use of ten frames has really made an impact.

Overall Unit Reflections: Things to Remember or Change for Next Year

We altered our pacing this year to reflect our essential learning standards. We have had three counting units and two units of composing and decomposing numbers. We worked with numbers up to 5 for most students. During the first addition and subtraction unit, we worked with numbers up to 5 for most students. We also have been using a subitizing routine since October. This intentional spiraling has had a clear impact since our results are much stronger this year than last. We would like to continue with this same pacing calendar next year.

Figure 4.10: Reflection and notes for kindergarten addition and subtraction to 10 unit.

team discussions as shared in this chapter. (See figure 1.2, page 11, for the template with directions.)

The addition and subtraction to 10 mathematics unit plan in figure 4.11, with its accompanying calendar showing daily learning targets and common assessments (see figure 4.5, page 69), scores high on the Mathematics Unit Planning Rubric in figure 2.2 (page 17). How will your team continue planning units for the year and document your discussions so each person on your team can learn from one unit to the next and one year to the next?

Conclusion

Although this chapter discusses only one exemplar of a kindergarten mathematics unit, each mathematics unit your team builds creates a foundational building block to effectively ensure student learning across your grade-level team. Your team's clarity will maximize individual teachers' instructional minutes and strengthen practices. Every member of your team and, more important, every student will benefit as you strive to achieve the self-efficacy promise that each and every student can learn the mathematics standards for kindergarten.

The next chapter shows the first-grade addition and subtraction to 20 unit plan example. Whether the standards you see in the following unit plan are a direct match to your state standards or not, consider the key ideas your students will be expected to learn next year in first grade along the foundations of addition and subtraction story arc for grades preK–2.

Unit: Kindergarten Addition and Subtraction to 10 Start Date: February 24 End Date: March 27 Total Number of Days: 24	
Essential Learning Standards	• I can quickly say how many dots I see. • I can make and break apart numbers to 10. • I can solve story problems. • I can show ways to make 10.
Prior Knowledge	**PreK and kindergarten (earlier in the year):** • Subitize images showing 1–5. • Count a set of 1–10 objects. • Join and separate up to 5. • Explore different ways to combine numbers to make 5.
Vocabulary and Notations	Zero through ten (Identify the numerals, and hear and say the name for each number from 0 to 10) Dot images Five and ten frames Add Subtract Story problem Notations: +, −, =, and pictures to represent joining and separating

Figure 4.11: Kindergarten addition and subtraction to 10 unit planner.

continued →

Resources and Activities	• Book 6, Lessons 1.1–1.4 and 2.1–2.8 • Sorting station • Mix and mingle: Find a partner with the same amount • One more, one less station • Create your own story problem with scenario mats • Compatible numbers • Ten-frame puzzles • Team-developed subitizing dot cards and finger flash cards • Bears in Caves: www.doe.virginia.gov/testing/sol/standards_docs/mathematics/2016/mip/index.shtml • Team-developed act-it-out problem solving • Ten Frame Addition task: www.illustrativemathematics.org
Tools and Technology	• Counters (bears, blocks, beads, cubes, and so on) • Linking cubes • Rekenreks • Five and ten frames • Part-part-whole mats • Number line • Dot cards • Dominoes • Dice or number cubes • Toy Theater virtual manipulatives: https://toytheater.com/category/teacher-tools/virtual-manipulatives • NCTM Illuminations, Ten Frame: www.nctm.org/Classroom-Resources/Illuminations/Interactives/Ten-Frame/ • Team-developed lessons using SMART Board

Reflection and Notes	When planning:
	
	• Continue to use our daily routine that we developed in the early fall and stations that allow for continued student practice independently or with teacher guidance.
	• We want to make sure to emphasize the language of joining and separating rather than focusing on the symbolic use of the plus, minus, and equal signs.
	  Examples:
	    ○ 2 and 6 is the same as 5 and 3
	    ○ 6 take away 1 is 5
	• Last year we had a lot of success using the act-it-out kits and story mats. Students solved given problems and created their own. We want to do this again and need time for students to create their own.
	• Using ten frames and our fingers are critical for developing the concept of 10. So, we need to make sure to intentionally plan for opportunities to utilize these tools. It will be important to observe who can subitize the frames and their own fingers rather than always having to rely on counting all or from 1.
	
	After the unit:
	
	• Since we now have a spreadsheet checklist to monitor subitizing, we were able to see quickly who was proficient, close to proficient, and far from proficient. We have several students ready for subitizing double images and more complex patterns and can determine at the next assessment window if they will be beyond proficient. We will reassess in three weeks after continued guided instruction and practice.
	• Our students who are still inconsistently counting one-to-one need the most extra time and support. We are putting all five students into one group. During math workshop, they will re-engage in counting, joining, and separating lessons three times per week for twelve to fifteen minutes.

Reflection and Notes	• Many students can solve problems in a variety of joining and separating contexts, but we are noticing that an area of weakness is recording their thinking. We are thinking about experimenting with this plan moving forward: 　○ Use iPads to record videos of students solving problems using tools, and share the videos with your class during guided instruction. 　○ Have the teacher scribe what the student is saying or doing using words, pictures, and/or numbers. 　○ Transition to the students representing thinking with words, pictures, or numbers to describe how they solved the problems. • Our results using the team-developed observation tool: **Making Tens Assessment** <table><tr><td>Strategy Used</td><td>Percent of Students</td></tr><tr><td>Immediate recall of tens</td><td>17%</td></tr><tr><td>Subitized an image or fingers</td><td>36%</td></tr><tr><td>Counting on from the larger number</td><td>20%</td></tr><tr><td>Counts all and starts at 1</td><td>18%</td></tr><tr><td>No access</td><td>9%</td></tr></table> We were so excited to see the number of students who were not having to rely on a counting-all strategy. It seems that our combination of subitizing routine and use of ten frames has really made an impact. Changes for next year: • We altered our pacing this year to reflect our essential learning standards. We have had three counting units and two units of composing and decomposing numbers. During the first addition and subtraction unit, we worked with numbers up to 5 for most students. We also have been using a subitizing routine since October. This intentional spiraling has had a clear impact since our results are much stronger this year than last. We would like to continue with this same pacing calendar next year.

CHAPTER 5

Grade 1 Unit:
Addition and Subtraction to 20

First grade continues the student learning story arc started in preK and kindergarten. In preK and kindergarten, students learned counting skills and subitized small images. In kindergarten, students composed and decomposed numbers to 10 and solved addition and subtraction stories by considering the concepts of joining and separating in real-life problems. Now, in first grade, students flexibly compose and decompose within 10 and, having learned the teen numbers in kindergarten, begin building strategies to add and subtract within 20. Students in first grade also make connections between the structured dot images and tools they are using to represent addition and subtraction using self-made pictures and numerical expressions and equations.

First grade is a time for you and your team to guide students in enriching their mathematics learning story, and to position their learning to provide a foundation for what they will need to know next year. Second-grade students will need to fluently add and subtract to 20 and develop efficient strategies to add and subtract within 100 and with special cases to 1,000. The understanding of tens and ones developed in first grade support the learning needed next year.

Since addition and subtraction is a considerable priority in the primary grades, it is likely your students will not be able to learn and master all concepts in a single unit. Therefore, your team will need to develop more than one math unit devoted to addition and subtraction during the school year. Your district proficiency map or pacing guide that identifies pacing and the placement of standards in each unit for the year will

provide clarity for your team. Working as a first-grade team, one of your goals is to build student confidence, self-efficacy, and a productive disposition with addition and subtraction based on your intentional unit design.

This chapter shares a mathematics unit exemplar for how your first-grade team might plan a mathematics unit using the essential standards related to addition and subtraction to 20. The standards that follow may or may not match your state standards exactly, but most likely they contain the key ideas of most of your standards. These standards were first shared in table P2.1 (page 37) and are labeled *standards 1.1–1.4.*

1.1.	**Fluently compose and decompose 10 with and without objects and pictures.**
1.2.	**Apply basic fact strategies to add and subtract within 20, including counting on, making 10 and decomposing a number leading to a 10, and using the relationship between addition and subtraction.**
1.3.	**Use addition and subtraction within 20 to solve word problems that involve joining, separating, comparing, and part-whole relationships with the unknowns in all positions.**
1.4.	Determine the unknown whole number in an addition or subtraction equation relating three whole numbers. *For example, $4 + ? = 13$, $8 = \boxed{} - 3$, $3 + 3 = ?$*

The bold standards reflect the need-to-know essential standards in the unit (see figure 2.3, page 19). These are the standards your team uses when creating common mid-unit assessments and uses first when addressing student gaps or extensions in learning. These more critical standards in the unit will be shared with you in either district documents or state, provincial or national guidelines. The bold standards are not, however, the only standards students will learn in the unit. The standard not in bold is the important-to-know standard and will also be included in your common end-of-unit assessment.

The distinction between the two sets of standards is the bold (need-to-know) standards incorporate the prior learning experiences from preK and kindergarten, and therefore, it is appropriate to expect a first grader to have mastery over these skills and concepts by the end of the year. By the end of first grade, students are expected to fluently add and subtract within 10 and apply what they know about addition, subtraction, and place value to solve larger sums and differences. However, the fourth non-bolded standard is also important, as students should learn to record addition and subtraction using symbols, and to show an understanding of the equals sign. Your first-grade team will design high-quality core instruction that develops the concepts of equality, reading equations, and finding missing numbers in equations, all of which will be continued into second grade. Therefore, your first-grade team's most pressing interventions and extensions relate to students' ability to compose and decompose numbers to 20 and interpret, solve, and represent various problem types.

Once your team has clarity about the standards in the unit and understands how they fit in the foundations of addition and subtraction story arc for a first grader, it is time for you to begin creating your unit plan. The Mathematics Unit Planner will guide your team and provide a location for you to record your agreements (see figure 1.2, page 11). Your team's work starts with generating essential learning standards in student-friendly language for assessment and reflection.

❶ Essential Learning Standards

Once your first-grade team has clarified the need-to-know and important-to-know standards in the

addition and subtraction to 20 unit, you can determine the essential learning standards. The essential learning standards are the driver for your common assessments and student reflections related to learning. They are written as *I can* statements and generated from the state standards students must learn in the unit. They form the daily learning targets for lessons. Your team clarifies the meaning of each by unwrapping the standards together.

What *exactly* do students have to know and be able to do to be proficient with the standards in the unit? As a team, use the team protocol to unwrap and make sense of mathematics standards to answer this critical question as shown in figure 2.4 (page 20). Completed first-grade templates for the need-to-know standards of the addition and subtraction to 20 unit appear in figures 5.1 (page 86), 5.2 (page 87), and 5.3 (page 89).

While unwrapping standard 1.1 in figure 5.1 (page 86), each teacher on your team will deepen his or her understanding of composing and decomposing numbers as it relates to student proficiency with addition and subtraction. Your team might discuss how students develop early arithmetic concepts and apply that knowledge to sums and differences within 10.

Young students first join quantities by counting from 1 while objects remain in constant view. Later, students can count imagined images, fingers, and objects, still starting at 1, but can make meaning without having to touch the concrete examples. Students then progress to being able to count forward from a number other than 1 (ideally starting with the greater of two given numbers when adding) and, finally, use known facts and numerical strategies that lead to immediate recall. Students' numeracy understanding is built on understanding the system of base ten, and therefore is a focus not only within this unit of study but in much of your team's first-grade mathematics units throughout the year.

Standard 1.2 (see figure 5.2, page 87) is related to standard 1.1 (see figure 5.1, page 86). Students will extend their understanding of adding to make 10 and subtracting from 10 to solving sums and differences within 20.

As you unwrap standard 1.2 (see figure 5.2, page 87), your team may discuss how the standard requires students to think flexibly and use multiple strategies. At this point, you may even determine the strategies you want to make sure all first graders learn and can use. You can discuss how to know whether or not students understand how to count on, make 10, and decompose to make a 10, along with other strategies chosen by your team. Your team may consult online resources, your curriculum materials, or kindergarten and second-grade teachers as you learn together how to expect students to develop mental strategies from a conceptual understanding of addition and subtraction. You might also discuss how to include subitizing as a strategy for students to use images to add and subtract, building on learning from kindergarten.

In this sample addition and subtraction to 20 unit, all four standards are intertwined, making it difficult to teach each in complete isolation. Understanding how to break apart 10 is directly related to developing flexible strategies with facts. Problem contexts serve as the vehicle for understanding joining and separating and give purpose for reasoning with number combinations. And, in order to ensure students do not develop misconceptions around the meaning of the equals sign (read as *equals* or *is the same as*), consider how your team will make intentional connections between standard 1.4 and standards 1.1–1.3 during instruction. Determine how students should be reading and recording thinking.

Standard 1.3 requires students to solve word problems using addition and subtraction. Your team may unwrap the standard using the process in figure 5.3 (page 89) as a model.

During the process of unwrapping standards like those shown in standard 1.1 (see figure 5.1, page 86), standard 1.2 (see figure 5.2, page 87), and standard 1.3 (see figure 5.3, page 89), it is helpful to consider how students are expected to show proficiency with the standards on your team's common end-of-unit assessment, ongoing assessments given throughout the year, or any school or district end-of-year assessment. A clear picture of the end goal can support your first-grade team as you generate ideas and navigate conversations that lead to being ready to complete the components of the unwrapping protocol, especially those related to tasks and student proficiency levels.

Since standards are often written formally, without much team time spent making sense of them, you and your teammates may interpret the standards differently. The process of circling verbs and underlining noun phrases is meant to bring a clarity and focus to what students must be able to do. Clarity comes from the meaningful conversations you have as a team in the process.

Standards 1.1–1.3 are the need-to-know standards in this addition and subtraction to 20 unit, but your team also builds a shared understanding of the important-to-know standard in the unit—standard 1.4 related to finding the unknown value in an addition or subtraction equation. Once the process of developing shared understanding is complete, your first-grade mathematics team combines information to generate the addition and subtraction to 20 unit essential learning standards and daily learning targets from the unwrapped standards (see figure 5.4, page 91). (See figure 2.5, page 22, for the template with directions.)

Your first-grade team can place the information in the center column of figure 5.4 (page 91) in the first row of the Mathematics Unit Planner as the essential learning standards (see figure 5.11, page 105).

Sometimes state standards are grouped together to form a student-friendly essential learning standard when they are closely aligned. However, grouping standards is not something needed in this unit because the essential learning standards are distinct and fall within the range of three to six essential learning standards for the unit. The daily learning targets share the story of the learning in the unit and are from the concepts and skills portion of the unwrapping work.

Both the essential learning standards and daily learning targets provide a resource for your team as you plan lessons and assessments. For your unit planning, the next step is to agree on the dates for common assessments and create the addition and subtraction to 20 learning story arc with daily learning targets on a calendar.

Unit: Grade 1—Addition and Subtraction to 20	

State Standard in the Unit:

1.1. (Fluently compose) and (decompose) 10 with and without objects and pictures.

Conceptual Understanding What do students need to know?	Procedural Knowledge and Skills What do students need to do?
• Composing 10 • Decomposing 10 • Number pairs that add to ten	• Fluently compose numbers to make 10. • Fluently decompose 10 into 2 numbers. • Given a set of objects or a number less than 10, find how many more are needed to make 10 by joining (adding). • Take 10 objects and separate them into 2 groups, saying how many are in each group and demonstrating an understanding that they make 10 together. • Determine all the different number pairs or combinations that make 10 using objects, fingers, pictures, or mental strategies.

Academic Vocabulary and Notations		
Add (+)	Subtract (−)	"Is the same as" or Equals (=)

Essential Learning Standards (In student-friendly language—I can . . .)	
• I can add to make 10.	• I can subtract from 10.

Proficiency Level of Understanding	
4 **Advanced**	Fluently compose and decompose numbers to 10 and greater than 10 with and without tools or drawings.
3 **Proficient**	Fluently compose and decompose numbers to 10 using objects, fingers, and pictures as well as without tools or drawings.
2 **Partial**	Use objects, fingers, or pictures to compose and decompose numbers to 10.
1 **Minimal**	With support, use objects, fingers, or pictures to compose and decompose numbers to 10.

Exemplar Tasks to Meet Standard:

Task 1—Tower to Ten

Give students two colors of linking cubes. Use dot dice or digit cards to generate a number. Students build that number using the first color and add on using the second color to make sums of 10.

Task 2—Apples and Bananas

Give students 10 red and 10 yellow counters. Challenge them to find all the ways they can make a total of 10 apples, bananas, or both. Ten frames could be used to support subitizing and fluently seeing combinations of 10.

Task 3—What's in the Cup?

Start with 10 objects shown to students. Put a few in a cup, and show the rest to the students. Students say how many are in the cup. This can be played in pairs, with students taking turns hiding a number of objects in the cup.

Task 4—What's My Number?

Tell students that you are thinking of a number. When your number is added to _____, you get 10. What is the number? Have students play the game in pairs, and then prove that they found the right number by drawing or using objects.

Figure 5.1: Unwrap and make sense of standard 1.1.

Unit: Grade 1—Addition and Subtraction to 20	
State Standard in the Unit:	
1.2. Apply basic fact strategies to add and subtract within 20, including counting on, making 10 and decomposing a number leading to a 10, and using the relationship between addition and subtraction.	

Conceptual Understanding **What do students need to know?**	**Procedural Knowledge and Skills** **What do students need to do?**
• Addition within 20 • Subtraction within 20 • Addition and subtraction strategies including the following: 　○ Counting on 　○ Making 10 (create a 10) 　○ Decomposing a number leading to a 10 　○ Relationship between addition and subtraction	• Add within 20 using strategies. • Subtract within 20 using strategies. • Apply addition and subtraction strategies such as the following: 　○ Count on or back 　○ Make 10 　○ Decompose or subtract to 10 　○ Relationship between addition and subtraction (for example, add up to solve a subtraction fact or equation with a missing addend)

Academic Vocabulary and Notations					
Add (+)	Subtract (−)	Sum	Difference	Equal (=)	Equation

Essential Learning Standard
(In student-friendly language—I can . . .)
• I can add and subtract numbers to 20 and explain my thinking. (Strategies may include counting on, counting back, making 10, and using doubles, among others.)

Proficiency Level of Understanding	
4 **Advanced**	Know addition and subtraction facts to 20, and apply this knowledge to think flexibly when adding three or more addends or finding larger sums or differences.
3 **Proficient**	Use fact strategies to add and subtract within 20 and show the thinking used (strategies include counting on, making 10, and decomposing to make a 10 as well as the relationship between addition and subtraction).
2 **Partial**	Use fact strategies to add and subtract within 10, but may struggle with larger facts to 20.
1 **Minimal**	Add or subtract with support, and rely mostly on a counts-all strategy.

Figure 5.2: Unwrap and make sense of standard 1.2.

continued →

Exemplar Tasks to Meet Standard:

Task 1: Count On—What Is the Sum?

Work with a partner. Roll two number cubes to generate numbers to add together. Partner A says the starting addend. Partner B counts on one more. Then partner A counts the next number, alternating back and forth until they count on to reach the sum. For example, if a 3 and a 5 are rolled, partner A can say, "Five." Partner B would say, "Six," and then partner A would say, "Seven," and partner B finally says, "Eight," the sum of the two numbers they rolled.

Task 2: Various Strategies—Double Ten Frames

Engage the class in number routines that encourage sharing different strategies for finding sums and differences on double ten frames. Manipulation of the dot images leads to mentally composing and decomposing numbers and the use of known facts.

Find the sum of 8 and 7.	Find the difference between 13 and 6.
Student A	**Student A**
I see 7 + 7 and 1 more makes 15.	I know 6 + 6 = 12. So, 6 + 7 must be 13.
Student B	**Student B**
I put 2 with the 8 to make 10. 10 and 5 is 15.	I took 3 off first to get back to 10. Then I took off 3 more and there were 7 left.

Task 3

Add or subtract and show how you know your answer is correct.

15 − 5	10 + 3
12 − 6	9 + 6
9 − 5	3 + 4

Unit: Grade 1—Addition and Subtraction to 20

State Standard in the Unit:

1.3. (Use) addition and subtraction within 20 to (solve) word problems that involve joining, separating, comparing, and part-whole relationships with the unknowns in all positions.

Conceptual Understanding What do students need to know?	Procedural Knowledge and Skills What do students need to do?

• Addition within 20
• Subtraction within 20
• Represent word problems in multiple ways such as with pictures, objects, or equations with the unknown in any position
• The meaning of addition and subtraction to apply to word problem contexts involving the following:
   ○ Joining
   ○ Separating
   ○ Comparing
   ○ Part-whole relationships
	• Solve word problems requiring addition and subtraction within 20.
	• Solve word problems involving the following:
	   ○ Joining
	   ○ Separating
	   ○ Comparing
	   ○ Part-whole relationships
	• Represent a word problem using tools, drawings, number lines, or equations.
	• Determine where the missing number is in the word problem story, and choose a strategy to solve the problem.

Academic Vocabulary and Notations	
Word problem or story problem	Difference
Add (+)	Equal (=)
Subtract (−)	Equation
Sum	

Essential Learning Standard (In student-friendly language—I can . . .)
• I can add and subtract to solve story problems and show my thinking.

Proficiency Level of Understanding	
4 **Advanced**	Interpret and solve one-step word problems with unknowns in different positions using strategies and recording work as an equation. May solve two-step word problems.
3 **Proficient**	Interpret and solve most one-step word problems with unknowns in different positions and show a strategy or record an equation.
2 **Partial**	Interpret and solve one-step word problems with unknowns in predictable positions and may show a strategy or record an equation.
1 **Minimal**	Solve one-step word problems with unknowns as the sum or difference with guided support to interpret the context.

Figure 5.3: Unwrap and make sense of standard 1.3.

continued →

Exemplar Tasks to Meet Standard:

Task 1—Part-Part-Whole

Problem A:

Ellie has 8 stickers. Her sister Sophie has 9 stickers.

How many stickers do they have all together?

Problem B:

Ellie has 9 stickers. Her sister Sophie has some stickers too. Together they have 17 stickers in all.

How many stickers does Sophie have?

Task 2—Start, Change, Result

Problem A:

Maddi is baking cookies. She baked 18 cookies. Her cousin Landon ate 6 cookies.

How many cookies does Maddi have left?

Problem B:

Maddi is baking cookies. She bakes 18 cookies. Her cousin Landon just ate some of her cookies. Now Maddi only has 12 cookies.

How many cookies did Landon eat?

Problem C:

Maddi is baking cookies. She has 12 cookies left after her cousin Landon ate 6 cookies.

How many cookies did Maddi have at the start?

Task 3—Compare

Problem A:

Anton and Eduardo are making towers with blocks. Anton made a tower with 11 blocks. Eduardo made a tower with 6 blocks.

How many fewer blocks did Eduardo use?

Problem B:

Anton and Eduardo are making towers with blocks. Anton has 11 blocks. Eduardo has 6 more blocks than Anton.

How many blocks does Eduardo have?

Formal Unit Standards (State Standard Language)	Essential Learning Standards for Assessment and Reflection (Student-Friendly Language)	Daily Learning Targets — What students must know and be able to do for each lesson (unwrapped standards) (Story Board Progression)
1.1. Fluently compose and decompose 10 with and without objects and pictures.	• I can add to make 10. • I can subtract from 10.	Students will be able to: • Fluently compose numbers to make 10. • Fluently decompose 10 into 2 numbers. • Given a set of objects or a number less than 10, find how many more are needed to make 10 by joining (adding). • Take 10 objects and separate them into 2 groups, saying how many are in each group and demonstrating an understanding that they make 10 together. • Determine all the different number pairs or combinations that make 10 using objects, fingers, pictures, or mental strategies.

1.2. Apply basic fact strategies to add and subtract within 20, including counting on, making 10 and decomposing a number leading to a 10, and using the relationship between addition and subtraction.	• I can add and subtract numbers to 20 and explain my thinking.	Students will be able to:
		• Add within 20 using strategies.
		• Subtract within 20 using strategies.
		• Apply addition and subtraction strategies such as—
		  ○ Count on or back
		  ○ Make 10
		  ○ Decompose or subtract to 10
		  ○ Relationship between addition and subtraction (for example, add up to solve a subtraction fact or equation with a missing addend)

1.3. Use addition and subtraction within 20 to solve word problems that involve joining, separating, comparing, and part-whole relationships with the unknowns in all positions.	• I can add and subtract to solve story problems and show my thinking.	Students will be able to:
		• Solve word problems requiring addition and subtraction within 20.
		• Solve word problems involving—
		  ○ Joining
		  ○ Separating
		  ○ Comparing
		  ○ Part-whole relationships
		• Represent a word problem using tools, drawings, number lines, or equations.
		• Determine where the missing number is in the word problem story, and choose a strategy to solve the problem.

1.4. Determine the unknown whole number in an addition or subtraction equation relating three whole numbers. *For example, $4 + ? = 13$, $8 = \boxed{} - 3$, $3 + 3 = ?$*	• I can find the missing number in an equation.	Students will be able to: • Find any missing number in an addition equation. • Find any missing number in a subtraction equation.

Figure 5.4: Grade 1 addition and subtraction to 20 unit standards, essential learning standards, and daily learning targets.

❷ Unit Calendar

The unit calendar includes common assessment dates and the student-friendly targets that help shape the story of learning that is about to take place. The team unit calendar is not meant to be a lockstep approach to teaching among team members. Rather, the goal is to have an idea of how long to spend on each essential learning standard and the general order of when to address learning targets.

The three bold standards in the unit will be used to create common mid-unit assessments. Your team may decide to have one common mid-unit assessment or several. Earlier in first grade, your team might use several days for ongoing assessments that include one-on-one interview or observational assessments. Whatever the type of common assessment, consider when these assessments should occur in the unit (preferably after learning has happened) for the most meaningful student and teacher reflection and next steps. Consider, too, when the unit must end and how many days to allocate to instruction and assessment. The common end-of-unit assessment will include all five of the essential learning standards in the unit. Also, are there any holidays, or should your team plan for flex days (days for re-engaging students in learning)?

One possible way to plan for student learning and common assessments appears in figure 5.5. The calendar identifies the daily learning targets and common assessments for each day of the addition and subtraction to 20 unit. (See figure 2.6, page 24, for the template with directions.)

If this is the first time your team is making the calendar, start with identifying the dates of your agreed-on common assessments in the unit. Next, work together as a team to plan the flow of the unit. Understand that through the reflection during and after each unit, the flow and storyline will become stronger and more precise each year.

Should your team decide ending dates need to change during a unit because you need more time to teach, it is important to communicate possible changes with one another. Consult your proficiency map or yearlong pacing guide to make sure you still have time for the remaining mathematics units. Record any changes in the Reflection and Notes portion of the Mathematics Unit Planner (see figure 1.2, page 11) to remember them for the next year.

Once your team has an agreed-on calendar and story for the unit of instruction, the next step is to discuss the prior knowledge students are expected to be proficient with before the unit of instruction begins.

❸ Prior Knowledge

Why is the addition and subtraction to 20 unit at this point in the year in first grade? What units have your first graders engaged in this year (or last) that may contribute to their understanding of addition and subtraction to 20 (such as counting, place value, and composing and decomposing numbers to 10)? During this part of unit planning, your team answers questions like these to identify the prior-knowledge standards from earlier first-grade units or from standards in kindergarten the current unit requires.

Figure 5.6 (page 94) shows the prior-knowledge standards for each essential learning standard in the unit. (See figure 2.7, page 25, for the template with directions.) Once your team identifies prior-knowledge standards and examples of each, you summarize each standard so it is student friendly in the Mathematics Unit Planner (see figure 1.2, page 11). The far right column in figure 5.6 matches the prior knowledge in the grade 1 addition and subtraction to 20 unit planner (see figure 5.11, page 105).

While your team makes sense of the prior-knowledge standards, you will also discuss the kindergarten strategies used to support student learning of addition and subtraction in first grade. How did students use ten frames for subitizing? How did students learn to compose and decompose numbers? What manipulatives and strategies helped students understand the meaning of addition and subtraction?

Consider how to use prior-knowledge standards to start your lessons by using tasks that connect to the day's learning target as Kanold, Kanold-McIntyre, et al. (2018) discuss in *Mathematics Instruction and Tasks in a PLC at Work*. (Visit **go.SolutionTree.com/ MathematicsatWork** for free reproducibles.) You can embed routines for developing number sense using quick image number talks with ten frames and other dot arrangements as lesson openers. You might also use story problems with sums and differences within

Monday	Tuesday	Wednesday	Thursday	Friday
2/3 Routine: Subitize dot images Lesson: Compose 10	2/4 Routine: Subitize dot images Lesson: Compose 10	2/5 Routine: Subitize dot images Lesson: Decompose 10	2/6 Routine: Subitize dot images Lesson: Compose and decompose 10	2/7 Addition story problems to 10 **Common Mid-Unit Assessment:** • I can add to make 10. • I can subtract from 10.
2/10 Add within 20 and addition story problems with an unknown sum	2/11 Add within 20 and addition story problems with an unknown sum	2/12 Subtract within 20 and subtraction story problems with an unknown difference	2/13 Subtract within 20 and subtraction story problems with an unknown difference	2/14 Centers: Add and subtract within 20 Lesson: Addition and subtraction story problems with unknowns in all places
2/17 Holiday: No School	2/18 Centers: Add and subtract within 20 Lesson: Addition and subtraction story problems with unknowns in all places	2/19 Centers: Add and subtract within 20 Lesson: Addition and subtraction story problems with unknowns in all places	2/20 Addition and subtraction story problems with unknowns in all places **Common Mid-Unit Assessment:** • I can add and subtract numbers to 20 and explain my thinking.	2/21 Flex day based on student needs
2/24 Find missing numbers in addition and subtraction equations and addition and subtraction story problems with unknowns in all places	2/25 **Common Mid-Unit Assessment:** • I can add and subtract to solve story problems and show my thinking.	2/26 Routine: Equality with missing numbers in equations Lesson: Addition and subtraction story problems with unknowns in all places	2/27 Routine: Equality with missing numbers in equations Lesson: Addition and subtraction story problems with unknowns in all places	2/28 Routine: Equality with missing numbers in equations Lesson: Addition and subtraction story problems with unknowns in all places
3/3 Review station centers: Making and breaking apart 10, adding and subtracting to 20, solving word problems, and finding missing numbers in equations	3/4 **Common End-of-Unit Assessment:** • I can add to make 10. • I can subtract from 10. • I can add and subtract numbers to 20 and explain my thinking. • I can add and subtract to solve story problems and show my thinking. • I can find a missing number in an equation.	3/5 **Common End-of-Unit Assessment:** • I can add to make 10. • I can subtract from 10. • I can add and subtract numbers to 20 and explain my thinking. • I can add and subtract to solve story problems and show my thinking. • I can find a missing number in an equation.		

Figure 5.5: Grade 1 addition and subtraction to 20 unit calendar.

Formal Unit Standards (State Standard Language)	Essential Learning Standards for Assessment and Reflection (Student-Friendly Language)	Prior-Knowledge Standards From Prior Grade Level, Course, or Unit	Prior-Knowledge Summary With Exemplars
1.1. Fluently compose and decompose 10 with and without objects and pictures.	• I can add to make 10. • I can subtract from 10.	**Kindergarten:** Subitize images 1–10. For any number from 1 to 9, find the number that makes 10 when added to the given number (for example, by using objects or drawings) and record the answer with a drawing or equation.	• Subitize images on a ten frame. How many dots? How many more to make 10? • Use objects, pictures, or fingers to add on to make 10. I have 4 balls. How many more balls do I need to have 10 balls? Use counters, a Rekenrek, or draw a picture to find the answer.
1.2. Apply basic fact strategies to add and subtract within 20, including counting on, making 10 and decomposing a number leading to a 10, and using the relationship between addition and subtraction.	• I can add and subtract numbers to 20 and explain my thinking.	**Kindergarten:** Compose and decompose numbers less than or equal to 10 in more than one way using objects, drawings, fingers, and verbal expressions (for example, 5 is 3 and 2 or 4 and 1).	• Compose and decompose numbers to 10. Jasmine has 8 flowers. Some are red and some are yellow. How many red flowers and yellow flowers could Jasmine have? What is a different combination of red and yellow flowers Jasmine could have?
1.3. Use addition and subtraction within 20 to solve word problems that involve joining, separating, comparing, and part-whole relationships with the unknowns in all positions.	• I can add and subtract to solve story problems and show my thinking.	**Kindergarten:** Represent various verbal problem contexts involving joining and separating numbers to 10.	• Solve addition and subtraction word problems to 10. We have 3 boys with red shirts today. (Have them stand.) We have 1 girl with a red shirt today. (Have her stand.) How many students have red shirts today in our class?
1.4. Determine the unknown whole number in an addition or subtraction equation relating three whole numbers. *For example,* $4 + ? = 13$, $8 = \boxed{} - 3$, $3 + 3 = ?$	• I can find the missing number in an equation.	**Kindergarten and Grade 1 (earlier in the year):** Begin to record addition and subtraction equations from various verbal problem contexts, pictures, and to find the total of an expression.	• Record addition and subtraction thinking using equations. Tina has 3 pencils. She buys 5 more pencils. Write an equation that shows how many pencils Tina has all together. Finish the equation: $4 + 2 = \boxed{}$

10 to see how students approach addition and subtraction tasks before growing the numbers. Your team may also want to create a short preassessment to determine whether students have learned sums and differences to 10.

Your team has now identified the prior knowledge students will use to make connection to new learning in the unit. Next, your team determines the mathematics language (vocabulary and symbols) you expect students to use when communicating their learning and thinking.

❹ Vocabulary and Notations

One of the process standards of mathematics calls for students to use appropriate academic language when discussing and writing mathematics. For your team to support students' use of the academic language in the unit, you and your team need to identify the mathematics vocabulary words, visuals that support learning the language, and any notations (symbols) students will need to hear, use, read, write, and speak to clearly communicate. Consider how students will learn the vocabulary and notations in real time through strong lesson design.

Figure 5.7 (page 96) shows a team protocol that includes visual vocabulary displays your team might consider for creating a word wall or anchor chart as first-grade students learn the words and notations in the addition and subtraction to 20 unit. (See figure 2.8, page 27, for the template with directions.) The words and notations are then listed on the Mathematics Unit Planner for the unit (see figure 5.11 on page 105).

Once your team identifies the words and symbols students need to communicate their thinking, you can discuss how to use sentence frames, word walls, and activities to have students practice and gain familiarity with the academic vocabulary and notations. Your team can also discuss how to best record students' oral explanations of addition and subtraction strategies that they share during number routines, daily lessons, and as part of any student-led closure to a lesson. Students need explicit modeling, practice, and accessible examples in order to transition from representing mathematical thinking with tools and drawings to recording ideas using numbers and equations using more formal notations.

In *Mathematics Instruction and Tasks in a PLC at Work* (Kanold, Kanold-McIntyre, et al., 2018), there are several ideas for how to infuse the learning of vocabulary and notations into daily lessons as a component of quality lesson design. (Visit **go.SolutionTree. com/MathematicsatWork** for free reproducibles.) Keep in mind, your team may find it helpful to connect with the kindergarten and second-grade teams to better align the vocabulary and notations students are expected to understand and use along the story arc of foundations of addition and subtraction. Together, your teams can determine common visuals, definitions, and displays that support student learning.

Your team's choice of mathematical tasks and activities is central to the learning of students, and your team's agreements for which to use in lessons mean first-grade students have equitable learning expectations. The next part of the Mathematics Unit Planner (see figure 1.2, page 11) asks you and your collaborative team to identify the resources and activities your team might use in the classroom.

❺ Resources and Activities

Understanding addition and subtraction are important concepts when developing flexibility with numbers and using numbers to describe a first-grader's world. Together, your team chooses both higher- and lower-level-cognitive-demand tasks for students to demonstrate their understanding of strategies to add and subtract to 20 and engage in word problems. What problem structures are most appropriate for first-grade students? What are the best types of tasks to use to develop both conceptual understanding, application, and procedural fluency dictated by the standards? As a first-grade collaborative team, you identify any common resources or activities that will effectively help every student learn the grade-level essential learning standards.

Once your team has clarity on the essential learning standards and examples of mathematical tasks to use for instruction and assessment, it is time to consider your resources. Your team can consider questions like the following.

- Which parts of our school-adopted textbooks or program correlate to the standards in the unit?

- Which are the best lessons or tasks to use in our books or program?

Unit: Grade 1—Addition and Subtraction to 20	
Vocabulary	**Definition, Explanation, Drawing, or Example**
Add	To join or put together Add Join together "2 and 3 is 5 altogether."
Subtract	To take away from, take apart, or compare Subtract Take apart "If I take 1 away from 4, I will still have 3 left."
Sum	The sum is the answer when adding numbers. Sum The answer in an addition problem What is the sum of 8 and 6? 14! 8 + 6 = 14
Difference	The difference is the answer when subtracting numbers. Difference The answer in a subtraction problem What is the difference between 8 and 6? 2! 8 − 6 = 2

Equal	When two amounts (or expressions) are the same value
	Equal Values that are the same [cubes] is the same as [cubes] $3 + 1 = 2 + 2$
Equation	A number sentence that shows two equal number expressions **Equation** $7 = 4 + 3$ $10 - 2 = 8$ $6 + 2 = 9 - 1$
Story problem or word problem	Math problem involving words and numbers **Story Problem** 3 birds were on a branch. 1 bird flew away. How many birds are left?

Notation	Words to Show How to Read the Notation	Example Showing How to Use the Notation in a Mathematics Expression or Equation
+	Plus or add	$3 + 2$
−	Minus, take away, or subtract	$10 - 4$
=	Is the same as (or equals)	$3 + 2 = 5$
Symbol to show an unknown to include: ___ or ? or ☐	Each symbol represents a missing value, so it is often read as "something" or "a number" (for example, 3 plus a number is the same as 5).	$3 + ? = 5$

Figure 5.7: Vocabulary and notations protocol for grade 1 addition and subtraction to 20 unit.

- Are there lessons or tasks to omit in a chapter or program because they don't match the standards in the unit?

- What ongoing centers or learning stations should we prepare to include?

- Is there a need for additional explorations, activities, or lessons because our books or program does not fully teach each essential learning standard? If so, what other resources should we use or develop?

Figure 5.8 shows possible answers to these questions and shares examples of lower- and higher-level-cognitive-demand tasks for the essential learning standards in the unit. (See figure 2.9, page 28, for the template with directions.) Some parts of the chart may be left blank because, for example, your first-grade team may decide no supplemental or online resources are necessary.

Your first-grade team should select a balance of higher- and lower-level-cognitive-demand tasks that match the rigor proficient students demonstrate, making sure to have the unknown in different places for the word problems involving addition and subtraction. Through this practice, you are contributing to a shared bank of resources. It is here—in the selection of resources—that the most significant teacher learning may occur as your team archives what to use for instruction from year to year. Your resources are intentionally kept, adjusted, or discarded based on the evidence of student learning collected by you and your team.

After your team plans the learning experiences and determines any common resources and activities to use in the unit, place the information in the Mathematics Unit Planner (see figure 5.11, page 105). Now your team has just one more part of the unit planner to agree on—the technology and tools students should use during instruction and assessment.

⑥ Tools and Technology

When planning for a unit on addition and subtraction to 20 in first grade, which tools or manipulatives are needed for meaningful explorations leading to conceptual understanding? How can tools or technology support and extend deeper student understanding or allow for opportunities to practice skills and concepts related to addition and subtraction?

Together, your team determines the tools and technology students should use for learning purposes. Tools are instruments used to employ a variety of strategies while students are learning or demonstrating learning. In first grade, tools are often manipulatives students use, graphic organizers, or number lines. Be sure to discuss which technology and tools can be used on common assessments and when students might need to minimize their use of the tool during instruction, if at all. It might be tempting to discuss strategies too. Remember, you can document strategies you discuss in the Reflection and Notes section of the Mathematics Unit Planner (see figure 1.2, page 11).

Your team may have access to computer programs designed to use visual models or games to help students build fluency with addition and subtraction. There are also virtual manipulatives on the Toy Theater website (https://toytheater.com/category/teacher-tools/virtual-manipulatives). Determine as a team any technology you want students to access across your first-grade team during the unit.

Figure 5.9 (page 100) shows an example of tools and technology your team could agree to use in the unit, the purpose of each tool, and whether you and your colleagues should use each one for instruction or common assessments (with an explanation, if needed). (See figure 2.10, page 30, for the template with directions.) Once your team has determined which tools and technology to use in the unit, add the information to the Tools and Technology section in the unit planner (see figure 5.11, page 105).

First-grade students need many experiences with concrete materials in order to build an understanding of concepts. This means your first-grade team might need to consider how tools will be managed in the classroom, determine how students will access tools during whole-group and small-group instruction, as well as during independent practice, and discuss how students will learn to select the tools needed during a lesson. From the tools, students learn to draw pictures to represent problems and finally record their work with equations. Also, explicit teaching and modeling may be necessary for students to effectively use technology.

Standard	Example	Higher-Level Task Example	Textbook Lessons	Projects, or Activities	Resources
I can add to make 10. I can subtract from 10.	Use a ten frame to add or subtract, How many more make ten? [ten frame] Take 3 away from 10. How many are left? [ten frame]	Find all the number pairs that add to 10. Prove you have found them all using pictures, numbers, or words.	Chapter 6, Lessons 6.3 and 6.4	Games as centers: • Rekenreks Make 10 • Go Fish for 10 • What's in the Cup? (counters) • Break a Train (linking cubes) • Give Me 10 • Find Pairs That Make 10 • Sorting sums: Greater than, less than, or equal to 10	Illustrative Mathematics: www.illustrativemathematics.org tasks • Making a Ten • Cave Game Subtraction Achieve the Core: https://achievethecore.org tasks • How Many Are Hiding? (10 cubes) • Snap It (10 cubes)
I can add and subtract numbers to 20 and explain my thinking.	Add or Subtract: $9 + 4 = ?$ $\Box + 6 = 12$ $11 - 2 = ?$	Carl says he can add $9 + 7$ because he can start with 9 and count on 7 more. He counts: 9, 10, 11, 12, 13, 14, 15, 16 and says the answer is 16. Is Carl correct? Explain by showing another way to find $9 + 7$.	Chapter 6, Lessons 6.5–6.8	Strategy Gala: Prove I am right with multiple strategies Ten Frames: Bridge to Ten game Doubles and Near Doubles Bingo	Achieve the Core: https://achievethecore.org tasks • How Many Are Hiding? (More than 10 cubes) • Snap It (More than 10 cubes)
I can add and subtract to solve story problems and show my thinking.	Charlotte has 8 pencils. She needs 12 pencils for a party. How many more pencils does Charlotte need?	Charlotte has these shirts in her closet: • 8 pink shirts • 6 blue shirts • 3 red shirts How many more pink shirts does Charlotte have than red shirts? How does the total of pink shirts compare to the total of blue and red shirts?	Chapter 7, Lessons 7.2–7.6	Act-it-out problem solving My Book of Story Problems	Illustrative Mathematics: www.illustrativemathematics.org tasks • The Very Hungry Caterpillar • At the Park
I can find the missing number in an equation.	What goes in the box to make this number sentence true? $5 + \Box = 9$	Lori says the question mark in the equation is 15. Is she correct? Explain why or why not. $10 + 5 = ? + 3$	Chapter 7, Lessons 7.1–7.2		Illustrative Mathematics: www.illustrativemathematics.org task • Equality Number Sentences

Figure 5.8: Resources and activities for grade 1 addition and subtraction to 20 unit.

Tool	Purpose	Instruction	Assessment
Counters (bears, two-colored counters, square tiles)	Conceptual understanding Exploration Justification	Show patterns Organize counting Model addition and subtraction	May be used for observational assessments or for team-specified common assessment questions.
Rekenreks	Conceptual understanding to compose and decompose numbers Exploration	Fact fluency Model equality	May be used for observational assessments or for team-specified common assessment questions.
Linking cubes	Conceptual understanding Exploration	Count and represent numbers Model addition and subtraction	May be used for observational assessments or for team-specified common assessment questions.
Balance scale	Conceptual understanding Exploration Justification	Model addition and subtraction with emphasis on equality	Not used on common assessments.
Base-ten blocks	Conceptual understanding Procedural understanding Representations	Count and represent numbers Early place-value concepts with tens and ones Model addition and subtraction	May be used for observational assessments or for team-specified common assessment questions.
Ten frames	Conceptual understanding Procedural understanding Fact fluency	Model addition and subtraction Subitize Make ten and learn teen numbers	May be used for observational assessments or for team-specified common assessment questions.
Part-part-whole mat	Conceptual understanding Exploration Justification Representations	Graphic organizer to compose and decompose numbers Make sense of word problems Model for addition and subtraction	May be used for observational assessments or for team-specified common assessment questions

Figure 5.9: Tools and technology for grade 1 addition and subtraction to 20 unit.

	Purpose	Instruction	Assessment
Dominoes ___ + ___ = ___ ___ + ___ = ___	Conceptual understanding Exploration Application	Add and subtract	Not used on common assessments unless it is part of the question.
Number line 1 2 3 4 5 6 7 8 9 10	Conceptual understanding Exploration Justification	Add and subtract	Student uses on team-agreed common assessment questions.
Technology	**Purpose**	**Instruction**	**Assessment**
Toy Theater virtual manipulatives: https:// toytheater.com/ category/teacher-tools/ virtual-manipulatives NCTM Illuminations, Ten Frame: www.nctm.org/ Classroom-Resources/ Illuminations/Interactives/ Ten-Frame Greg Tang Math, Math Limbo: https://gregtangmath .com/mathlimbo	Conceptual understanding Exploration Representations	Fact recall model Model addition and subtraction Problem solving Equality	Not used on common assessments.
Team-developed lessons using SMART Board	Exploration Representations	Fact recall model Model addition and subtraction Problem solving Equality	Not used on common assessments.

Your team has thoughtfully answered the first PLC at Work critical question, *What do we want all students to know and be able to do?* related to addition and subtraction to 20. Your team has clearly articulated the standards, chosen the tasks, and selected the tools needed in the unit. The final part of the Mathematics Unit Planner (see figure 1.2, page 11) provides space for you to record reflection and notes for future reference, either while teaching the unit or after it ends.

❼ Reflection and Notes

Your first-grade team most likely engaged in many rich and meaningful conversations as you completed protocols to plan your addition and subtraction to 20 unit. Along the way, you may have determined mathematical strategies to use when supporting student learning that can be recorded in the Reflection and Notes row of the unit plan.

During and after the unit, your team can reflect on instructional and assessment practices that worked well for student learning or identify changes to make in the future. Recording that information in this last row of the unit planner allows your team to learn from this year's experiences to better impact student learning of the essential learning standards in this unit next year.

This systematic process of unit design would not be complete without including a protocol for reflection.

Figure 5.10 shows a completed team reflection on the first-grade addition and subtraction to 20 unit. (See figure 2.11, page 31, for the template with directions.)

The protocol in figure 5.10 serves as an archive of your team successes, a living plan of next steps, and a dialogue about what is currently working or not working for your first-grade students. As you build trust among your team, consider the following guiding questions for supporting transparent and honest dialogue after your common end-of-unit assessment.

- Where in the data do you see a trend to celebrate?

- After looking at your classroom data, what questions would you ask your teammates?

- What would you like to know more about to support one another's mathematical teaching practices?

- Where in the data do you see evidence of a need to adjust your team's approach to teaching the standards in the unit?

Questions such as these encourage open reflection on what your team's data is telling you and help you to focus your instructional plan moving forward.

Your team has now identified the essential learning standards from the state standards in the first-grade addition and subtraction to 20 unit. You have worked together to agree on and clarify the prior knowledge, vocabulary and notations, resources and activities, and tools and technology. Along the way and after the unit ended, you have recorded reflections and notes. Your team has now successfully generated the information needed to complete the Mathematics Unit Planner for your addition and subtraction to 20 unit.

Grade 1 Addition and Subtraction to 20 Unit Planner

Your team discussions during the planning of the addition and subtraction to 20 unit strengthen your daily lesson design and common assessments. Figure

5.11 (page 105) shows the completed Mathematics Unit Planner for the first-grade addition and subtraction to 20 unit, summarizing your team discussions as shared in this chapter. (See figure 1.2, page 11, for the template with directions.)

The addition and subtraction to 20 unit planner in figure 5.11 (page 105), with its accompanying calendar showing daily learning targets and common assessments (see figure 5.5, page 93), scores high on the Mathematics Unit Planning Rubric in figure 2.2 (page 17). How will your team continue planning units for the year and document your discussions so your team can learn from them from one unit to the next and one year to the next? How does each of your team mathematics unit plans score against the rubric in figure 2.2 (page 17)? Your challenge as a team is to continue planning for each unit to strengthen both student and teacher learning.

Conclusion

Although this is only one exemplar of a first-grade unit for mathematics, each mathematics unit your team builds will create a foundational building block for your team to effectively ensure the learning of students across your grade-level team. Together, your clarity will maximize your instructional minutes and strengthen your practices. Every member of your team and, more important, every student will benefit as you strive to achieve the self-efficacy promise that each and every student can learn the mathematics standards for first grade.

The next chapter shows the grade 2 multidigit addition and subtraction unit example. Read through the example to see possible standards teachers expect students to learn next year as a continuation of the foundations of addition and subtraction story arc for grades preK–2.

Essential Learning Standard	Notes When Planning: What to Emphasize or Remember for Lessons and Assessments in the Unit	Team Reflections After the Unit
I can add to make 10. I can subtract from 10.	Use multiple games to reinforce number pairs to 10. Introduce and rotate them. Tools, ten frames, and part-part-whole mats should be available as supports during guided instruction and independent practice. We need to develop an assessment that we can use to monitor tens fluency progress over time.	Rotating the games went well and helped with engagement. Most of us kept a game in the rotation for about a week or so. They love Go Fish, so we kept that one in longer. $6 + 4$ and $7 + 3$ are the most difficult for our students, and only about 50% of students are applying tens addition facts to subtraction. If we continue to keep the games in our workshop and do some targeted guided practice, we can reassess in four weeks to see how our students are progressing.
I can add and subtract numbers to 20 and explain my thinking.	Use number talks as part of our daily routine, and create anchor charts for student reference and reinforcement. Examples:	We need to remember to always ask students which strategy they used and support their ability to explain and then record how they are solving problems. Take a few pictures of some of the better anchor charts we have created during this unit to use later this year or next. Students need more work with the Make a 10 strategy. We need to use more tools.

Make Ten	Use Doubles	Subtract to Ten
$9 + 3 = ?$ $\wedge$ $1\ \ 2$	$6 + 7 = ?$ $\wedge$ $6\ \ 1$	$15 - 8 = ?$ $\wedge$ $5\ \ 3$
$(9 + 1) + 2 = ?$	$(6 + 6) + 1 = ?$	$(15 - 5) - 3 = ?$
$10 + 2 = 12$	$12 + 1 = 13$	$10 - 3 = 7$

Plan to continue to include games in centers. These strategies also develop when solving story problems.

We had success in the past making connections by selecting students to share in this order:

1. Concrete and counting-all strategies
2. Pictorial and counting-on strategies
3. Numerical representations and use of known facts

Make anchor charts so that we can support student progression through these strategies.

Figure 5.10: Reflection and notes for grade 1 addition and subtraction to 20 unit.

continued →

Essential Learning Standard	Notes When Planning: What to Emphasize or Remember for Lessons and Assessments in the Unit	Team Reflections After the Unit
I can add and subtract to solve story problems and show my thinking.	We are planning to work through the problem types in this order during guided instruction. We know some students might be ready for the more complex problem types a little sooner than others: 1. Join and separate (result unknown) Part-part-whole (whole unknown) 2. Part-part-whole (part unknown) Join and separate (change unknown) Join and separate (start unknown) 3. Comparison problems • Ask students to retell the story in their own words before doing anything else. Students should be able to explain the story before guessing what to do! • Have students act out the story if there is an action or change involved. • Use pictures or manipulatives with the part-part-whole mat for support. • Encourage the use of efficient strategies to solve the word problems so the unit holds together.	Watch out that we don't teach "key words" as the way to know whether to add or subtract. One teacher shared her process for problem solving. During the first read-aloud of the problem: • Visualize while listening or reading. • Talk to a neighbor, and restate in own words. During the second read-aloud of the problem: • Visualize while listening or reading. • Act it out with tools. • Represent thinking with pictures, numbers, or equations.
I can find the missing number in an equation.	We want to ensure that our students have experiences with concrete objects and balance scales that connect to equations as they find a missing number. Have students come up with two different ways to add to 10 (reinforce the first standard) and show that the two expressions are equal because they are both 10 (for example, $8 + 2 = 5 + 5$). Use tools to find missing numbers in equations. Link the equations to adding and subtracting within 20 and story problems.	Some students are trying to memorize the pattern of an equation or think the equal sign represents the answer. We need to have them think about what is the same instead. Be sure to show the equal sign in different locations such as $5 = 3 + ?$ and read it as "5 is the same as 3 and a number."

Overall Unit Reflections: Things to Remember or Change for Next Year

How can we write common assessments to evaluate and note student strategies? We are encouraging students at the end of the unit to use their best strategy, and it would be important to know to what degree they are proficient. We like the idea of developing a rubric next time to help us understand their needs and know where to go next.

The games and activities went very well. Students have a solid understanding of 10, although decomposing numbers to make a 10 was tricky for most students. We need to find time during our next unit to continue this work. Could we possibly develop a routine and learning station to add to our workshop games?

Unit: Grade 1 Addition and Subtraction to 20 **Start Date:** February 3 **End Date:** March 5 **Total Number of Days:** 22	
Essential Learning Standards	• I can add to make 10. • I can subtract from 10. • I can add and subtract numbers to 20 and explain my thinking. (For example, by counting on, counting back, making 10, and using doubles) • I can add and subtract to solve story problems and show my thinking. • I can find the missing number in an equation.
Prior Knowledge	**Kindergarten:** • Subitize images on a ten frame. • Use objects, pictures, or fingers to add on to make 10. • Compose and decompose numbers to 10. • Solve addition and subtraction word problems to 10. **Kindergarten and Grade 1 (earlier units):** • Record addition and subtraction thinking using equations.
Vocabulary and Notations	Add Subtract Sum Difference Equal Equation Story problem or word problem Notations: + (add), − (subtract), = (is the same as or equals) Symbols for an unknown such as: _____ , ?, or ☐

Resources and Activities	• Grade 1 textbook: Chapter 6, Lessons 6.3–6.8
	• Grade 1 textbook: Chapter 7, Lessons 7.1–7.6
	• Games as centers:
	   ◦ Rekenreks Make 10
	   ◦ Go Fish for 10
	   ◦ What's in the Cup? (counters)
	   ◦ Break a Train (linking cubes)
	   ◦ Give Me 10
	   ◦ Find Pairs That Make 10
	• Sorting sums: Greater than, less than, or equal to 10
	• Strategy Gala: Prove I am right with multiple strategies
	• Ten Frames: Bridge to Ten game
	• Doubles and Near Doubles Bingo
	• Act-it-out problem solving
	• My Book of Story Problems
	• www.illustrativemathematics.org: Making a Ten, Cave Game Subtraction, The Very Hungry Caterpillar, At the Park, and Equality Number Sentences
	• https://achievethecore.org: How Many Are Hiding? (10 and more cubes) and Snap It (10 and more cubes)

Figure 5.11: Grade 1 addition and subtraction to 20 unit planner.

continued →

Tools and Technology	• Counters (bears, two-colored counters, square tiles) • Rekenreks • Linking cubes • Balance scale • Base-ten blocks • Ten frames • Part-part-whole mat • Dominoes • Number line • Toy Theater virtual manipulatives: https://toytheater.com/category/teacher-tools/virtual-manipulatives • NCTM Illuminations, Ten Frame: www.nctm.org/Classroom-Resources/Illuminations/Interactives/Ten-Frame • Greg Tang Math, Math Limbo: https://gregtangmath.com/mathlimbo • Team-developed lessons using SMART Board
Reflection and Notes	When planning: • Use multiple games to reinforce number pairs to 10. Introduce and rotate them. Tools, ten frames, and part-part-whole mats should be available as supports during guided instruction and independent practice. • We need to develop an assessment that we can use to monitor tens fluency progress over time. • Use number talks as part of our daily routine, and create anchor charts for student reference and reinforcement. For example—

Make Ten	Use Doubles	Subtract to Ten
$9 + 3 = ?$ 　∧ 　1　2 $(9 + 1) + 2 = ?$ $10 + 2 = 12$	$6 + 7 = ?$ 　∧ 　6　1 $(6 + 6) + 1 = ?$ $12 + 1 = 13$	$15 - 8 = ?$ 　∧ 　5　3 $(15 - 5) - 3 = ?$ $10 - 3 = 7$

• Plan to continue to include games in centers. These strategies also develop when solving story problems.
• In the past, we had success making connections by selecting students to share strategies in the following order:

1. Concrete and counting-all strategies

2. Pictorial and counting-on strategies

3. Numerical representations and use of known facts

• Make anchor charts so that we can support student progression through these strategies.
• We are planning to work through the problem types in this order during guided instruction. We know some students might be ready for the more complex problem types a little sooner than others:

1. Join and separate (result unknown)
   Part-part-whole (whole unknown)

2. Part-part-whole (part unknown)
   Join and separate (change unknown)
   Join and separate (start unknown)

3. Comparison problems

| **Reflection and Notes** | <ul><li>Ask students to retell the story in their own words before doing anything else. Students should be able to explain the story before guessing what to do!</li><li>Have students act out the story if there is an action or change involved.</li><li>Use pictures or manipulatives with a part-part-whole mat for support.</li><li>Encourage the use of efficient strategies to solve the word problems so the unit holds together.</li><li>We want to ensure that our students have experiences with concrete objects and balance scales that connect to equations as they find a missing number.</li><li>Have students come up with two different ways to add to 10 (reinforce first standard) and show that the two expressions are equal because they are both 10. For example, 8 + 2 = 5 + 5.</li><li>Use tools to find missing numbers in equations. Link the equations to adding and subtracting within 20 and story problems.</li></ul>After the unit:<ul><li>Rotating the games went well and helped with engagement. Most of us kept a game in the rotation for about a week or so. They love Go Fish, so we kept that one in longer.</li><li>6 + 4 and 7 + 3 are the most difficult for our students, and only about 50% of students are applying tens addition facts to subtraction. If we continue to keep the games in our workshop and do some targeted guided practice, we can reassess in four weeks to see how our students are progressing.</li><li>We need to remember to always ask students which strategy they used and support their ability to explain and then record how they are solving problems.</li><li>Take a few pictures of some of the better anchor charts we have created during this unit to use later this year or next.</li><li>Students need more work with the Make a 10 strategy. We need to use more tools.</li><li>Watch out that we don't teach "key words" as the way to know whether to add or subtract.</li><li>One teacher shared her process for problem solving—<ul><li>During the first read-aloud of the problem:<ul><li>Visualize while listening or reading.</li><li>Talk to a neighbor, and restate in own words.</li></ul></li><li>During the second read-aloud of the problem:<ul><li>Visualize while listening or reading.</li><li>Act it out with tools.</li><li>Represent thinking with pictures, numbers, or equations.</li></ul></li></ul></li><li>Some students are trying to memorize the pattern of an equation or think the equal sign means the answer. We need to have them think about what is the same instead. Be sure to show the equal sign in different locations such as 5 = 3 + ? and read it as "5 is the same as 3 and a number."</li></ul>Changes for next year:<ul><li>How can we write common assessments to evaluate and note student strategies? We are encouraging students at the end of the unit to use their best strategy, and it would be important to know to what degree they are proficient. We like the idea of developing a rubric next time to help us understand their needs and know where to go next.</li><li>The games and activities went very well. Students have a solid understanding of 10, although decomposing numbers to make a 10 was tricky for most students. We need to find time during our next unit to continue this work. Could we possibly develop a routine and learning station to add to our workshop games?</li></ul> |

CHAPTER 6

Grade 2 Unit:
Multidigit Addition and Subtraction

Second grade completes the grades preK–2 arc for the foundations of addition and subtraction learning story. This story began in preK with counting skills such as the forward rote counting sequence, one-to-one correspondence when counting a set of objects, and subitizing up to five-dot images.

In kindergarten, students subitize larger dot images, expand their counting skills, join and separate physical models, and engage in verbal problem solving with picture representations and some written equations or expressions.

In first grade, students begin to develop fluency with addition and subtraction within 10 and use strategies to add and subtract within 20 and solve more complex one-step word problems (with unknowns in all positions). Students also work with addition and subtraction with special cases within 100.

The foundational work related to addition and subtraction concepts in grades preK–1 leads to second graders learning strategies for two-digit addition and subtraction and solving both one and two-step word problems. Students even use manipulatives and pictures to add and subtract within 1,000. Next year, in third grade, students will expand their understanding of the place-value system to numbers beyond 1,000 and become more fluent with addition and subtraction of larger numbers using various algorithms based on place value. A student's journey from understanding counting and cardinality, addition and subtraction, and the base-ten system leads to a fourth-grade student who is finally expected to fully master the addition and subtraction algorithm and have quick strategies to use when adding and subtracting with large numbers.

In second grade, a significant portion of instructional time will focus on the essential learning standards for building place-value understanding of the base-ten system to include writing numbers in more than one way using hundreds, tens, and ones. Students will also spend significant time working towards fluency with addition and subtraction to 20 and developing a conceptual understanding of addition and subtraction with regrouping of two-digit numbers, while exploring sums and differences within 1,000. As your second-grade team plans units related to multidigit addition and subtraction, start with clarifying what students are expected to know and be able to do.

It is too difficult to ensure students learn all the concepts related to addition and subtraction in second grade within a single unit. Therefore, your team will need more than one unit of instruction for teaching multidigit addition and subtraction during the school year. Your district proficiency map or pacing guide identifies pacing and the placement of standards in each unit for the year and will provide clarity for your team. Working as a second-grade team, one of your goals is to build student confidence, self-efficacy, and a productive disposition based on your intentional unit design.

This chapter shares a mathematics unit example for how your second-grade team might plan a unit using the essential standards related to multidigit addition and subtraction. The standards that follow may or may not match your state standards, but most likely they contain the key concepts. Your team will have been working to have students learn some of these and other standards related to addition and subtraction prior to starting this unit. This will not be, for example, the first or only time students continue to build accurate, efficient, and flexible strategies to fluently add and subtract within 20. Knowing fluency to 20 benefits students when finding larger sums and differences within the unit means the standard is addressed as a routine in this unit. The following standards were first shared in table P2.1 (page 37) and are labeled *standards 2.1–2.4*.

2.1.	**Fluently add and subtract within 20 using mental strategies leading to immediate recall.**
2.2.	Use concrete and pictorial models to represent numbers up to 1,000 in more than one way as sums of hundreds, tens, and ones.
2.3.	**Estimate and find multidigit sums and differences within 100, with and without regrouping, using various methods based on place value.**
2.4.	**Use addition and subtraction within 100 to represent and solve one- and two-step word problems involving joining, separating, comparing, and part-whole relationships with the unknowns in all positions.**

The bold standards reflect the need-to-know essential standards in the unit (see figure 2.3, page 19). These are the standards your team uses when creating common mid-unit assessments and uses first when addressing student gaps or extensions in learning. These more critical standards in the unit will be shared with you in either district documents or state, provincial, or national guidelines. They are not, however, the only standards students will learn in the unit. The non-bolded standard is the important-to-know standard and will be included in your common end-of-unit assessment.

The distinction between the two sets of standards for this unit is that the bold standards incorporate prior learning experiences from preK, kindergarten, and first grade, and therefore, it is appropriate to expect a second grader would have mastery over these skills and concepts by the end of the year. By the end of second grade, students are expected to fluently add and subtract within 20 and find sums and differences to 100 using strategies based on place value. These bold need-to-know standards require that students understand equality and can apply their understanding of addition and subtraction to word problems.

The non-bolded standard is also important. Students in second grade develop a deeper understanding of the base-ten system and addition and subtraction with various regrouping strategies. How well do students understand there are different groupings of tens and ones to make many numbers? How flexible does their number reasoning need to be to add and subtract?

Students will continue to add and subtract with special cases to 1,000 in a later unit (and in third grade), so proficiency with standard 2.2 is not expected yet, but some knowledge of this standard will strengthen adding and subtracting using place value in this unit. The most pressing interventions and extensions center on students' ability to compose and decompose numbers to 20; interpret, solve, and represent various word problem types; and build an understanding of regrouping when adding or subtracting two-digit numbers.

Once your team has clarity about the standards in the unit and how they fit in the multidigit addition and subtraction story arc of a second grader, it is time for you to begin creating your unit plan. The Mathematics Unit Planner will guide your team and provide a location for you to record your agreements (see figure 1.2, page 11). Your team's work starts with generating essential learning standards in student-friendly language for assessment and reflection.

❶ Essential Learning Standards

Once your second-grade team has clarified the need-to-know and important-to-know standards in the multidigit addition and subtraction unit, you can determine the essential learning standards. The essential learning standards are the driver for your common assessments and student reflections related to learning. They are written as *I can* statements and generated from the state standards students must learn in the unit and form the daily learning targets for lessons. Your team clarifies the meaning of each essential standard by unwrapping the standards together.

So, what *exactly* do students have to know and be able to do to be proficient with the standards in the unit? Together, use the team protocol to unwrap and make sense of mathematics standards to answer this critical question as shown in figure 2.4 (page 20). Completed templates for the need-to-know standards appear in figures 6.1, 6.2 (page 112), and 6.3 (page 114).

Unit: Grade 2—Multidigit Addition and Subtraction	
State Standard in the Unit:	
2.1. Fluently add and subtract within 20 using mental strategies leading to immediate recall.	

Conceptual Understanding What do students need to know?	Procedural Knowledge and Skills What do students need to do?
• Mental addition to 20 strategies • Mental subtraction within 20 strategies • Immediate recall of sums to 20 • Immediate recall of differences within 20	• Fluently add within 20. • Fluently subtract within 20. • Use mental strategies to add and subtract (for example, make ten, doubles, and near doubles). • Grow to immediate recall of basic facts within 20.

Academic Vocabulary and Notations					
Add (+)	Subtract (−)	Sum	Difference	Equal (=)	Equations

Essential Learning Standards (In student-friendly language—I can . . .)	
• I can quickly add within 20.	• I can quickly subtract within 20.

Proficiency Level of Understanding	
4 **Advanced**	Immediately recall all addition and subtraction facts within 20 and begin to apply this knowledge to think flexibly when solving multidigit addition and subtraction problems.
3 **Proficient**	Fluently add and subtract within 20 using efficient mental strategies (such as using a smaller known fact) with accuracy and flexibility when a fact cannot be recalled.
2 **Partial**	Fluently add and subtract within 10 and, rather than consistently applying known facts, may use a count-on or count-back strategy when a fact cannot be recalled.
1 **Minimal**	Does not yet efficiently add and subtract and relies mostly on a counts-all strategy and the use of manipulatives.

Exemplar Task to Meet Standard:

Task—Strategy Checklist

Show the student a flash card with the addition or subtraction expression shown on the checklist. Score the student response using the following scoring key. (Enter a number for each fact.)

4: Immediate recall

3: Uses a known fact like tens or doubles to compose or decompose

2: Counts on or back

1: Counts all or by ones to determine the sum or difference

Student Names	9 + 7	4 + 8	7 + 6	16 − 8	14 − 5	11 − 7

Figure 6.1: Unwrap and make sense of standard 2.1.

Unit: Grade 2—Multidigit Addition and Subtraction

State Standard in the Unit:

2.3. (Estimate) and (find) multidigit sums and differences within 100, with and without regrouping, (using) various methods based on place value.

Conceptual Understanding What do students need to know?	Procedural Knowledge and Skills What do students need to do?

• Multidigit sums within 100
• Multidigit differences within 100
• Regrouping tens and ones
• Estimation of sums
• Estimation of differences
• Addition and subtraction methods based on a place-value understanding of tens and ones
	• Determine multidigit sums and differences with and without regrouping using various methods such as the following:
	   ○ Represent addition and subtraction with base-ten tools and models
	   ○ Decompose both addends and then add tens with tens and ones with ones
	   ○ Count on or count back by tens and ones
	• Estimate sums and differences within 100.

Academic Vocabulary and Notations	
Place value	Regroup
Add (+)	Estimate
Subtract (–)	Equal (=)
Sums	Equation
Differences	

Essential Learning Standards (In student-friendly language—I can . . .)
• I can estimate sums and differences within 100 and explain my thinking. • I can add and subtract within 100 and explain my thinking.

Proficiency Level of Understanding	
4 **Advanced**	Add and subtract within 100 or more using and explaining efficient numerical strategies. Closely estimate sums and differences with accurate reasoning.
3 **Proficient**	Add and subtract within 100 using various strategies based on place value. Estimate sums and differences, and explain the reasoning involved.
2 **Partial**	Add and subtract numbers to 100 with some inaccuracies using a place-value understanding that relies mostly on base-ten tools, charts, and picture models. Estimates may be far from the actual sum or difference.
1 **Minimal**	With support, use place-value understanding or a base-ten strategy to add and subtract within 100 and often rely on a counts-by-one strategy. Estimates are often far from the actual sum or difference.

Exemplar Tasks to Meet Standard:

Task 1—Add To or Subtract From Base-Ten Models

a. Braden started with the following base-ten blocks. Now he has 90.

What number did Braden add?

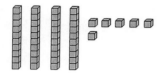

b. Nick has the following base-ten blocks. If Nick removes 17 blocks, how many will he still have?

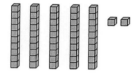

Task 2—Race to Zero

Start with 100. Roll a die to determine how much to subtract. Model using base-ten blocks and a place-value chart. Record the results on the following chart.

Number Rolled	Find the Difference	Did You Break Apart a Ten?	
5	100 − 5 = 95	☑ Yes	☐ No
2	95 − 2 = 93	☐ Yes	☑ No
6	93 − 6 = 87	☑ Yes	☐ No
		☐ Yes	☐ No
		☐ Yes	☐ No

Task 3—Open Number Line

Camden is 32 years old. His mom is 58 years old. How much older is Camden's mom than Camden? Use the number line to solve the problem.

Task 4—Determine the Difference

Herbie and Nathan each pulled a two-digit number out of a bag. Herbie pulled 27, and Nathan pulled 68. Herbie says the difference between the two numbers is 41. Do you agree or disagree?

Build a model and write an equation to prove if Herbie is correct or incorrect.

Task 5—Estimate: How Close?

Determine which sum or difference best estimates the answer. Then find the actual answer.

	Circle the best answer.	Find the sum or difference, and show your work.
25 + 36	Sum is closest to: 50 60	25 + 36 = ?
75 − 67	Difference is closest to: 10 20	75 − 67 = ?

Figure 6.2: Unwrap and make sense of standard 2.3.

Unit: Grade 2—Multidigit Addition and Subtraction

State Standard in the Unit:

2.4. Use addition and subtraction within 100 to solve and represent one- and two-step word problems involving joining, separating, comparing, and part-whole relationships with the unknowns in all positions.

Conceptual Understanding What do students need to know?	Procedural Knowledge and Skills What do students need to do?

• Addition within 100
• Subtraction within 100
• One-step word problems
• Two-step word problems
• Variety of word problem types
   ○ Joining
   ○ Separating
   ○ Comparing
   ○ Part-whole relationships
• Unknowns in all positions when solving word problems
   ○ Part: 5 + _____ = 13
   ○ Part: _____ + 8 = 16
   ○ Part: 7 = 10 = _____
   ○ Whole: _____ 35 – 12
	• Add and subtract within 100 to solve:
	   ○ One-step word problems
	   ○ Two-step word problems
	• Solve word problems involving:
	   ○ Joining
	   ○ Separating
	   ○ Comparing
	   ○ Part-whole relationship
	• Use physical tools, drawings, number lines, and equations to determine solutions.
	• Show thinking used to solve one- and two-step word problems.
	• Write equations that can be used to represent and solve word problems.
	• Determine if an answer is reasonable by estimating and checking work.

Academic Vocabulary and Notations					
Add (+)	Subtract (−)	Sum	Difference	Equals (=)	Equation

Essential Learning Standard (In student-friendly language—I can . . .)
• I can add and subtract to solve word problems and show my thinking.

Proficiency Level of Understanding	
4 **Advanced**	Solve one-step word problems and non-scaffolded two-step word problems with unknowns in different positions. Given a range of possible answers, create a one- or two-step word problem with a solution in the given range.
3 **Proficient**	Solve one-step word problems and two-step word problems with unknowns in different positions.
2 **Partial**	Solve one-step word problems and scaffolded two-step word problems with unknowns in predictable positions.
1 **Minimal**	Solve one-step word problems with unknowns in predictable positions with guided support to interpret the context.

Exemplar Tasks to Meet Standard:

Task 1—Varied One-Step Problem Types

a. Judy bought 42 cookies for the winter party. People ate 34 cookies at the party. How many cookies does Judy still have?

b. Tom built a tower using 61 blocks. Dan built a tower using 43 blocks. How many more blocks did Tom use to build his tower than Dan?

c. Kyle has 18 markers in his backpack. He finds more markers in his desk. Now Kyle has 35 markers altogether. How many markers did Kyle find in his desk?

Task 2—Two-Step Word Problems

a. Tim walks to the park. He sees 15 birds, 32 squirrels, and 10 dogs. How many more squirrels did Tim see than birds and dogs put together?

b. Jen, Suzy, and Amy earn an allowance for household chores. Suzy has 35 cents, and Amy has 27 cents. Together, all three girls have a total of 99 cents. How much money does Jen have?

Figure 6.3: Unwrap and make sense of standard 2.4.

Sometimes mathematics standards are written in ways that can lead you and your teammates to varied interpretations. The process of circling verbs and underlining noun phrases is meant to bring a clarity and focus to what students must be able to do. Questions during your team discussions as you consider standard 2.1 might include the following.

- What experiences should a second grader have in developing fluency strategies (add and subtract efficiently, flexibly, and accurately)?

- How will our team, during instruction, teach students how to use and explain strategies when a fact cannot be recalled such as using known facts related to doubles and tens?

- Rather than relying on timed tests, what will our process be for assessing and monitoring fluency so that we have a true understanding of our students' needs and levels of proficiency?

- How have we built in routines so far this year to support fact fluency with addition and subtraction, and how will we continue and grow routines during this unit?

The strategy checklist shared as an exemplar task in figure 6.1 (page 111) includes a scoring key for recording how efficiently a student recalls each fact. While the checklist is not an exhaustive list of addition and subtraction facts to 20, it is a large enough sample to determine a student's preferred method and level of proficiency. A team-developed checklist such as this could be used over time to monitor a student's progress in developing fluency with addition and subtraction to 20.

Standards 2.2 and 2.3 are intentionally included together in this unit to illustrate how they are connected, even though standard 2.2 in not yet a need-to-know standard. Building, representing, and naming multidigit numbers should precede and coincide with addition and subtraction of numbers to 100 because it develops a deeper conceptual understanding of digits and place value needed for addition and subtraction. Representing 35 as three tens and five ones is a common model your team can use. However, being able to represent 35 as two tens and fifteen ones and knowing it represents the same value as 3 tens and 5 ones is a key concept in overcoming misconceptions with subtraction by regrouping.

The second need-to-know standard, standard 2.3, is shown in figure 6.2. (page 112).

During the process of unwrapping standards like those shown in figures 6.1 (page 111) and 6.2 (page 112), your team can discuss how students are expected to show proficiency with each standard on your common end-of-unit assessment or any end-of-year assessment given in second grade. A clear picture of the end goal can support your grade-level team as you generate ideas and navigate conversations that prepare you to complete the components of the unwrapping protocol, especially those related to tasks and student proficiency levels. It is not yet expected that students have proficiency with the addition and subtraction standard algorithm, but rather that they can use place value to develop efficient and accurate procedures to add and subtract within 100 while showing their reasoning.

Standard 2.4, the culminating standard in this unit, is shown in figure 6.3 (page 114). It is not important for students to know whether a word problem has one or two steps, but rather that they can plan a solution strategy and justify their reasoning, regardless of the number of steps they ultimately use. Students must ask, "Does my answer make sense?" The knowledge and skills students gained previously will be applied in the lessons, tasks, and activities that engage students in solving one- and two-step word problems.

Standards 2.1, 2.3, and 2.4 are the need-to-know standards in this multidigit addition and subtraction unit. Your team will similarly build a shared understanding of the other important-to-know standard in the unit—standard 2.2 related to representing numbers to 1,000 as various sums of hundreds, tens, and ones. Once complete, your second-grade mathematics team combines this information to generate the multidigit addition and subtraction unit essential learning standards and daily learning targets (see figure 6.4). (See figure 2.5, page 22, for the template with directions.)

Your second-grade team can copy the information from the center column of figure 6.4 into the first row of the Mathematics Unit Planner as the essential learning standards (see figure 6.11, page 129).

Sometimes, when state standards are closely aligned, they are grouped together to form a single student-friendly essential learning standard. However, grouping standards was not something needed in this unit because the essential learning standards are distinct and fall within the targeted range of three to six standards for the unit. The daily learning targets share the story of the learning in the unit and are from the concepts and skills portion of the unwrapping work.

Both the essential learning standards and daily learning targets provide resources for your team as you plan your lessons and assessments. For your unit planning, the next step is to add the dates for common assessments to the calendar and create the multidigit addition and subtraction learning story arc with daily learning targets.

❷ Unit Calendar

Now that your second-grade team has clarified the standards students will be learning in the multidigit addition and subtraction unit, you can consider pacing, common assessment dates, and the daily learning targets to address to maximize student learning. The unit calendar is not meant to be a lockstep approach to teaching among team members. Rather the goal is to have an idea of how long to spend on each essential learning standard and the general order of when to address learning targets.

Your team will use the three bold standards in the unit to create common mid-unit assessments. You may decide to have one mid-unit common assessment or several. Consider when they should occur during the unit (preferably after learning has happened) for the most meaningful student and teacher reflection and next steps. Consider, too, when the unit must end and how many days to allocate to instruction and assessment. Allow time for holidays, professional development days, or flex days (time allocated for re-engaging students in learning), if needed. The common end-of-unit assessment will include all six of the essential learning standards in the unit.

One possible way to plan for student learning and common assessments appears in figure 6.5 (page 118). This second-grade unit is later in the school year with an understanding that students have been working on fact fluency to 20 all year, so it is a routine and may be checked one more time at the beginning of the unit. Similarly, students have worked on one- and two-step word problems with numbers to 20 in a previous second-grade unit. The calendar in figure 6.5 (page 118) identifies the daily learning targets and common assessments for the multidigit addition and subtraction unit. (See figure 2.6, page 24, for the template with directions.)

If this is the first time your team is making the calendar, start with identifying the dates of your agreed-on common assessments in the unit. Next, work together as a team to plan the flow of the unit, but understand that through your team's reflection during and after each unit, the flow and storyline will become stronger and more precise each year.

Should your team decide ending dates need to change during a unit, be sure to communicate those possible changes with one another. Consult your proficiency map or yearlong pacing guide to ensure there is still time for the remaining mathematics units. Record any changes in the Reflection and Notes portion of the

Formal Unit Standards (State Standard Language)	Essential Learning Standards for Assessment and Reflection (Student-Friendly Language)	Daily Learning Targets What students must know and be able to do for each lesson (unwrapped standards) (Story Board Progression)
2.1. Fluently add and subtract within 20 using mental strategies leading to immediate recall.	• I can quickly add within 20. • I can quickly subtract within 20.	Students will be able to: • Fluently add within 20 • Fluently subtract within 20 • Use mental strategies to add and subtract (for example, make ten, doubles, and near doubles) • Grow to immediate recall of basic facts within 20
2.2. Use concrete and pictorial models to represent numbers up to 1,000 in more than one way as sums of hundreds, tens, and ones.	• I can represent numbers in more than one way using hundreds, tens, and ones.	Students will be able to: • Represent numbers using concrete and pictorial models showing hundreds, tens, and ones • Make connections between written three-digit numbers and models of hundreds, tens, and ones • Break apart numbers in more than one way as sums of hundreds, tens, and ones

2.3. Estimate and find multidigit sums and differences within 100, with and without regrouping, using various methods based on place value.	• I can estimate sums and differences within 100 and explain my thinking.
	• I can add and subtract within 100 and explain my thinking.
		Students will be able to:
		• Determine multidigit sums and differences with and without regrouping using various methods such as—
		  o Representing addition and subtraction with base-ten tools and models
		  o Decomposing both addends and then add the tens with the tens and the ones with the ones
		  o Count on or count back by tens and ones
		• Estimate sums and differences within 100

2.4. Use addition and subtraction within 100 to represent and solve one- and two-step word problems involving joining, separating, comparing, and part-whole relationships with the unknowns in all positions.	• I can add and subtract to solve word problems and show my thinking.	Students will be able to:
		• Add and subtract within 100 to solve—
		  o One-step word problems
		  o Two-step word problems
		• Solve word problems involving—
		  o Joining
		  o Separating
		  o Comparing
		  o Part-whole relationship
		• Use physical tools, drawings, number lines, and equations to determine solutions
		• Show thinking used to solve one- and two-step word problems
		• Write equations that can be used to represent and solve word problems
		• Determine if an answer is reasonable by estimating and checking work

Figure 6.4: Grade 2 multidigit addition and subtraction unit standards, essential learning standards, and daily learning targets.

Monday	Tuesday	Wednesday	Thursday	Friday
2/10 Routine: Fact fluency and equality Lesson: Represent numbers using base-ten pieces and pictures as combinations of hundreds, tens, and ones	2/11 Routine: Fact fluency and equality Lesson: Represent numbers in more than one way using hundreds, tens, and ones	2/12 Routine: Fact fluency and equality Lesson: Represent numbers in more than one way using hundreds, tens, and ones	2/13 Routine: Fact fluency and equality Lesson: Determine the number represented by various amounts of hundreds, tens, and ones	2/14 Routine: Fact fluency and equality Lesson: Represent numbers in more than one way using hundreds, tens, and ones **Common Mid-Unit Assessment:** • I can quickly add within 20. • I can quickly subtract within 20.
2/17 Student holiday Teacher planning day	2/18 Routine: Fact fluency and equality Lesson: One-step word problems	2/19 Routine: Fact fluency and equality Lesson: One-step word problems	2/20 Routine: Multidigit computation Lesson: One-step word problems	2/21 Routine: Multidigit computation Lesson: One-step word problems
2/24 Routine: Multidigit computation Lesson: One-step word problems	2/25 **Common Mid-Unit Assessment:** • I can add and subtract to solve word problems and show my thinking. (Focus on one-step word problems)	2/26 Routine: Multidigit computation and estimation Lesson: Two-step word problems	2/27 Routine: Multidigit computation and estimation Lesson: Two-step word problems	2/28 Routine: Multidigit computation and estimation Lesson: Two-step word problems
3/3 Routine: Multidigit computation Lesson: Two-step word problems **Common Mid-Unit Assessment:** • I can estimate sums and differences within 100 and explain my thinking. • I can add and subtract within 100 and explain my thinking. • I can add and subtract to solve word problems and show my thinking. (Focus on two-step word problems)	3/4 Flex day based on student needs	3/5 Routine: Multidigit computation and estimation Lesson: Word problems with one- or two-steps	3/6 Review Day Stations: (1) fact fluency within 20, (2) show different combinations of hundreds, tens, and ones to represent a number, (3) add and subtract within 100 using strategies based on place value, (4) one-step word problems, and (5) two-step word problems	3/7 **End-of-Unit Assessment:** • I can quickly add within 20. • I can quickly subtract within 20. • I can represent numbers in more than one way using hundreds, tens, and ones. • I can estimate sums and differences within 100 and explain my thinking. • I can add and subtract within 100 and explain my thinking. • I can add and subtract to solve word problems and show my thinking.

Figure 6.5: Grade 2 multidigit addition and subtraction unit calendar.

Mathematics Unit Planner (see figure 1.2, page 11) to remember them for the next year.

Once your team has an agreed-on calendar and story for the unit of instruction, the next step is to discuss the prior knowledge students are expected to be proficient with before the unit of instruction begins.

❸ Prior Knowledge

Why is the multidigit addition and subtraction unit at this time of the year? What units have your second graders engaged in this year (or last) that may contribute to their understanding of addition and subtraction with larger numbers and one- and two-step word problems? During this part of the unit planning, your team answers questions like these to identify prerequisite content knowledge and skills students need to access the second-grade standards in the current unit.

Figure 6.6 (page 120) is a completed example that identifies the skills and prior-knowledge standards from earlier second-grade units or from first grade. (See figure 2.7, page 25, for the template with directions.) Once your team identifies the prior-knowledge standards, you should follow the protocol and summarize the standard, so it is student friendly in the Mathematics Unit Planner (see figure 1.2, page 11). The last column in figure 6.6 (page 120) matches the prior knowledge in the grade 2 multidigit addition and subtraction unit planner shown in figure 6.11 (page 129).

Start your lessons by using tasks that connect to the day's learning target as Kanold, Kanold-McIntyre, et al. (2018) discuss in *Mathematics Instruction and Tasks in a PLC at Work*. (Visit **go.SolutionTree.com/ MathematicsatWork** for free reproducibles.) You might make the connections using routines or during the start of the heart of your daily lesson. In the multidigit addition and subtraction unit, fluently adding and subtracting within 10 (and 20) is important prior knowledge. You can embed routines (as shown in the calendar) for developing number sense using number talks as lesson openers. Your team may also want to create a short preassessment that members can use to determine students' prior knowledge proficiency with multidigit addition and subtraction and word problems if you do not readily have the information from previous units.

After you and your team identity the prior knowledge needed for the unit, the next task for your team to address in the Mathematics Unit Planner is the mathematics vocabulary and notations students need to learn and use throughout the unit.

❹ Vocabulary and Notations

One of the process standards of mathematics calls for students to use appropriate academic language when discussing mathematics. To support students' use of the academic language, you and your team will need to identify the mathematics vocabulary words, visuals that support learning the language, and any notations (symbols) students will need to precisely use, read, write, hear, and speak to clearly communicate. Consider how students will learn the vocabulary and notations in real time through strong lesson design.

Figure 6.7 (page 121) shares a team protocol your team might also consider using for creating a word wall or anchor chart as second-grade students learn the words and notations in the multidigit addition and subtraction unit. (See figure 2.8, page 27, for the template with directions.) The words and notations are then listed in the Mathematics Unit Planner (see figure 6.11 on page 129).

Once your team identifies the words and notations for the unit, you can discuss how to use sentence frames, word walls, and activities to have students practice and gain familiarity with the academic vocabulary and notations. Your team can also discuss how to best record students' oral explanations of addition and subtraction strategies they share during daily number routines, lessons, and student-led closure to lessons. Students need explicit modeling, practice, and accessible examples in order to transition from representing mathematical thinking with tools and drawings to recording ideas using numbers and equations. Discuss how students will practice reading numbers and symbols in equations to make sense of what is being asked of them to find and so they can explain their reasoning using numbers and symbols with each other.

Mathematics Instruction and Tasks in a PLC at Work (Kanold, Kanold-McIntyre, et al., 2018) offers several ideas for how to infuse the learning of vocabulary and notations into daily lessons as a component of

Formal Unit Standards (State Standard Language)	Essential Learning Standards for Assessment and Reflection (Student-Friendly Language)	Prior-Knowledge Standards From Prior Grade Level, Course, or Unit	Prior-Knowledge Summary With Exemplars
2.1. Fluently add and subtract within 20 using mental strategies leading to immediate recall.	• I can quickly add within 20. • I can quickly subtract within 20.	**Grade 1:** Fluently compose and decompose 10 with and without objects and pictures. Apply basic fact strategies to add and subtract within 20, including counting on, making 10, and decomposing a number leading to a 10, and using the relationship between addition and subtraction.	• Compose and decompose within 10 quickly. Add: 2 + 5 Subtract: 10 – 3 • Use strategies to add and subtract within 20. Show how to find each sum or difference. 8 + 7 = ? 14 – 9 = ?
2.2. Use concrete and pictorial models to represent numbers up to 1,000 in more than one way as sums of hundreds, tens, and ones.	• I can represent numbers in more than one way using hundreds, tens, and ones.	**Grade 1:** Group a collection of objects into tens and ones, and write the corresponding number.	• Tell the number of tens and ones in a number. Show 32 two different ways using groups of tens and ones.
2.3. Estimate and find multidigit sums and differences within 100, with and without regrouping, using various methods based on place value.	• I can estimate sums and differences within 100 and explain my thinking. • I can add and subtract within 100 and explain my thinking.	**Grade 1:** Apply basic fact strategies to add and subtract within 20, including counting on, making 10, and decomposing a number leading to a 10, and using the relationship between addition and subtraction. Add two-digit by one-digit numbers within 100, with and without regrouping, using various methods based on place value.	• Use strategies to add and subtract within 20. Fluency assessment: Record students' strategy for each fact. 5 + 6 15 – 9 9 + 3 Scoring rubric: 4—Immediate recall 3—Uses a known fact 2—Counts on 1—Counts all (may include objects and fingers) • Add two-digit by one-digit numbers within 100 using different strategies. Solve and show your thinking: 34 + 8 = ?
2.4. Use addition and subtraction within 100 to represent and solve one- and two-step word problems involving joining, separating, comparing, and part-whole relationships with the unknowns in all positions.	• I can add and subtract to solve word problems and show my thinking.	**Grade 1:** Use addition and subtraction within 20 to solve word problems that involve joining, separating, comparing, and part-whole relationships with the unknowns in all positions.	• Solve word problems using addition or subtraction within 20 with unknowns in all positions. Charlie has 13 apples. He needs 15 apples for soccer practice. How many more apples does Charlie need?

Figure 6.6: Prior-knowledge standards for grade 2 multidigit addition and subtraction unit.

Unit: Grade 2—Multidigit Addition and Subtraction	
Vocabulary	**Definition, Explanation, Drawing, or Example**
Add	To join or put together Add Join together "2 and 3 is 5 altogether."
Subtract	To take away from, take apart, or compare Subtract Take apart "If I take 1 away from 4, I will still have 3 left."
Sum	The sum is the answer when adding numbers. Sum The answer in an addition problem What is the sum of 8 and 6? 14! 8 + 6 = 14
Difference	The difference is the answer when subtracting numbers. Difference The answer in a subtraction problem What is the difference between 8 and 6? 2! 8 − 6 = 2

Figure 6.7: Vocabulary and notations protocol for grade 2 multidigit addition and subtraction unit.

continued →

Equation	A number sentence that shows two equal expressions Equation 7 = 4 + 3 10 – 2 = 8 6 + 2 = 9 – 1
Equal	When two amounts (or expressions) are the same value Equal Values that are the same is the same as 3 + 1 = 2 + 2
Place value	The numerical value that a digit has given its place in the number Place value | Hundreds	Tens	Ones
---	---	---
100s	10s	1s	
Digit	The numerals from 0 to 9: 0, 1, 2, 3, 4, 5, 6, 7, 8, 9 Digits have different values depending on their placement in a number. Digit The value of the digit 3 in 437 is 30.

Estimate	An estimate is an informed guess at an answer.
	An estimate in computation may be found by rounding, by using front-end digits, by clustering, or by using compatible numbers to compute.

Estimate

"68 is close to 70.
23 is close to 20.

So the sum is about 90."

Notation	Words to Show How to Read the Notation	Example Showing How to Use the Notation in a Mathematics Expression or Equation
Expanded form: (200 + 30 + 5) (2 hundreds + 3 tens + 5 ones)	Two hundred plus thirty plus five Or Two hundreds plus 3 tens plus 5 ones	Show how to write 235 using hundreds, tens, and ones: 200 + 30 + 5
+	Plus or add	32 + 56
−	Minus, take away, or subtract	100 − 40
=	Equals or is the same as	63 + 17 = 80

quality lesson design. (Visit **go.SolutionTree.com/ MathematicsatWork** for free reproducibles.) Keep in mind, your team will find it helpful to connect with the first- and third-grade teams to align vocabulary and notations to grow student learning.

The next component of the unit planner outlines the instructional resources and activities your team might use in the classroom. Determining key resources, activities, and tasks as a team is central for delivering a guaranteed and viable curriculum to all learners. In this section of the unit planner, you and your collaborative team will identify the tasks, portions of lessons in curriculum materials, and supplemental resources needed for students to learn during the multidigit addition and subtraction unit.

❺ Resources and Activities

Together, your team chooses both higher- and lower-level-cognitive-demand tasks that students engage in to demonstrate their understanding of multidigit addition and subtraction. Including a wide range of addition and subtraction problem structures and contexts throughout each lesson is a priority for students in second grade. Which one- and two-step problem structures are students in second grade expected to master? What are the best types of tasks to develop conceptual understanding, application, and procedural fluency dictated by the standards? As a second-grade collaborative team, you identify any common resources or activities that will effectively help every student learn the grade-level essential learning standards in the unit, which your team will record in the template for the tool shown in figure 6.8 (page 124).

Once your team has clarity on the essential learning standards and examples of mathematical tasks to use for instruction and assessment, it is time to consider your resources. Your team might consider the following questions.

Essential Learning Standard	Lower-Level Task Example	Higher-Level Task Example	School-Adopted Textbook Lessons	Explorations, Projects, or Activities	Supplemental or Online Resources
I can quickly add within 20. I can quickly subtract within 20.	What goes into the blank to make each statement true? $9 + 9 =$ ___ ___ $= 7 + 3$ $13 - 6 =$ ___	Name pairs of numbers that have a sum of 15. Do you have all the combinations? Explain how you know.	District-Adopted Fluency Program Number Talks	Double Dice Plus One game Double ten-frame images Missing addends	Achieve the Core: https://achievethecore.org/page/2948/fluency-resources-for-grade-level-routines • Fluency Resources for Grade-Level Routines
I can represent numbers in more than one way using hundreds, tens, and ones.	Write the number that is shown in expanded form. $90 + 2$ $100 + 30 + 5$ $200 + 70 + 1$	Kevin, James, and Abe are having a contest to see who can make the largest number. Who wins? Defend your answer. Kevin: $220 + 15 + 2$ James: 249 Abe: 24 tens and 12 ones	Chapter 3, Lesson 3.7 Chapter 7, Lesson 7.2	Base-ten picture cards mix and match Base-ten riddles Ways to make a number	Illustrative Mathematics: www.illustrativemathematics.org Tasks • Bundling and Unbundling • Regrouping • Making 124
I can estimate sums and differences within 100 and explain my thinking. I can add and subtract within 100 and explain my thinking.	$15 = ? - 75.$ What is the value of the missing number? What is the difference between 72 and 39? Is the sum $32 + 19$ best estimated with the number 40, 50, or 60?	Jayden solved $68 - 28 = \square$ using the following strategy. $61 - 28 = ?$ $60 - 20 = 40$ $8 - 1 = 7$ The difference is 47. Is she correct or incorrect? How do you know? Is $70 - 42$ less than 50 or greater than 50? Explain how you know without finding the exact answer.	Chapter 6, Lessons 6.1–6.3	Compatible numbers task Tiered addition and subtraction Race to a Flat Race to Zero	Figure 3.11 in *Engage in the Mathematical Practices* (Norris & Schuhl, 2016); see go.SolutionTree.com /MathematicsatWork • Grade 2 Make Suggestions Example
I can add and subtract to solve word problems and show my thinking.	Derick read for 26 minutes, and Beth read for 57 minutes. How much longer did Beth read than Derick? Carli read 23 pages in her new book yesterday, 30 pages this morning, and 20 pages this afternoon. How many total pages has Carli read in her new book?	Lisa is making cupcakes for a party. So far, she has 36 vanilla cupcakes. Lisa made 25 more chocolate cupcakes than vanilla. If she has 90 guests coming to the party, does she have enough cupcakes for everyone to have at least one? How do you know?	Chapter 6, Lessons 6.4–6.10	Act-it-out problem solving Numberless word problems Visualizing task Create Your Own Story Problem station	

Figure 6.8: Resources and activities for grade 2 multidigit addition and subtraction unit.

- Which parts of our school-adopted textbooks correlate to the standards in the unit?

- Which are the best lessons or tasks to use in our books?

- Are there lessons or tasks to omit in a chapter because they don't match the standards in the unit?

- What ongoing centers or stations should we include?

- Is there a need for additional explorations, activities, or lessons because our book does not fully teach each essential learning standard? If so, what other resources should we use or develop?

Figure 6.8 shows possible answers to these questions and shares examples of lower- and higher-level-cognitive-demand tasks for the essential learning standards in the unit. (See figure 2.9, page 28, for the template with directions.) Some parts of the chart may be left blank because, for example, your second-grade team may decide no supplemental or online resources are necessary or available.

Your second-grade team should select a balance of higher- and lower-level-cognitive-demand tasks that match the rigor demonstrated by students considered proficient. Through this practice, you are contributing to a shared bank of resources. It is here—in the selection of resources—that the most significant teacher learning may occur as your team archives what to use for instruction from year to year. Your resources are intentionally kept, adjusted, or discarded based on the evidence of student learning you and your team collect.

After the learning experiences are planned and your team has determined any common resources and activities to use in the unit, place the information in the Mathematics Unit Planner (see figure 6.11, page 129). Now you are left with one more part of the unit planner to agree on—the technology and tools students should use during instruction and assessment.

❻ Tools and Technology

When planning for a unit on multidigit addition and subtraction in second grade, which tools or manipulatives are needed for meaningful explorations leading to conceptual understanding? How might tools or technology support extending deeper student understanding or allow for opportunities for students to practice the skills and concepts they are learning?

Together, your team determines the tools and technology students should use for learning purposes. Tools are instruments used to employ a variety of strategies while learning or demonstrating learning such as base-ten pieces, manipulatives, and number lines. Be sure to discuss which technology and tools students can use on common assessments and when students might need to minimize their use of the tool during instruction, if at all. It might be tempting to discuss strategies too (how students will use the tools or other addition and subtraction strategies). Your team can document strategies discussed in the Reflection and Notes section of the Mathematics Unit Planner (see figure 1.2, page 11).

Your team may have access to computer programs designed to use visual models or games to help students build fluency with addition and subtraction. There are also virtual manipulatives on the Toy Theater website (https://toytheater.com/category/teacher-tools/virtual-manipulatives). Determine as a team any technology you want students to access across your second-grade team during the unit.

Figure 6.9 (page 126) shows example tools and technology your team could agree to use in the unit, the purpose of each, and whether you and your colleagues should use each one for instruction or common assessments with an explanation, if needed. (See figure 2.10, page 30, for the template with directions.) Once your team has determined which tools and technology to use in the unit, add the agreed-on information to the Tools and Technology section in the Mathematics Unit Planner (see figure 6.11, page 129).

Second-grade students need many experiences with concrete materials in order to build an understanding of concepts. Your team might need to consider how tools will be managed in the classroom, determine how students will access tools during whole-group and small-group instruction, as well as during independent practice, and discuss how students will choose tools to use when needed. Consider how to explicitly teach and model for students the effective use of any tools and technology used during the unit.

Your team has thoughtfully answered PLC at Work critical question 1, *What do we want all students to*

Tool	Purpose	Instruction	Assessment
Counters	Conceptual understanding Exploration Developing fluency	Fact fluency Model equality	May be used for team-specified common assessment questions.
Rekenreks	Conceptual understanding Exploration	Fact fluency Model equality	Not used on common assessments.
Linking cubes	Conceptual understanding Exploration	Count and represent numbers Model addition and subtraction with and without regrouping	May be used for team-specified common assessment questions.
Base-ten blocks	Conceptual understanding Procedural understanding Modeling	Count and represent numbers Model addition and subtraction with and without regrouping	May be used for team-specified common assessment questions.
Ten frames	Conceptual understanding Representations Developing fluency	Fact fluency strategies Model equality	Not used on common assessments.
Hundreds chart	Exploration Conceptual understanding Procedural understanding Justification	Count forward and back Model addition and subtraction with and without regrouping	May be used for team-specified common assessment questions.
Place-value chart	Exploration Conceptual understanding Procedural understanding Justification	Count and represent numbers Connect place value to multidigit addition and subtraction	May be used for team-specified common assessment questions.
Open number line $15 + 39$ or	Conceptual understanding Application Justification	Add and subtract Jump method Show thinking using tens and ones for adding and subtracting	Student may use when solving questions on a common assessment.

Calculator	Exploration Verification	Use with solving word problems or to check answers, as needed	Not used on common assessments.
Technology	**Purpose**	**Instruction**	**Assessment**
National Library of Virtual Manipulatives: nlvm.usu.edu/ en/nav/vlibrary.html Math Playground: www. mathplayground.com/ GrandSlamMath1.html Arcademics: www. arcademics.com/games/alien Greg Tang Math: https:// gregtangmath.com/mathlimbo	Conceptual understanding Exploration Representations	Fact recall model Modeling and relating addition and subtraction Problem solving Equality	Not applicable
Team-developed lessons using SMART Board	Exploration Representations		Not used on common assessments.

Figure 6.9: Tools and technology for grade 2 multidigit addition and subtractions unit.

know and be able to do? related to multidigit addition and subtraction. Your team has clearly articulated the standards, chosen the tasks, and selected the tools needed in the unit. The final part of the Mathematics Unit Planner (see figure 1.2, page 11) provides space to record reflection and notes for future reference, either while teaching the unit or after it ends.

❼ Reflection and Notes

Your second-grade team most likely engaged in many rich and meaningful conversations as you completed protocols to plan the multidigit addition and subtraction unit. Along the way, you and your team may have determined mathematical strategies to use when supporting student learning. Your team can record observations and insights in the Reflection and Notes row of the unit planner.

During and after the unit, your team can reflect on instructional and assessment practices that worked well for student learning or identify changes to make in the future. Recording that information in this last row of the unit planner allows your team to learn from this year's experiences to better impact student learning of the essential learning standards in this unit next year.

Figure 6.10 (page 128) shows a completed example of team reflection and notes for the grade 2 multidigit addition and subtraction unit. (See figure 2.11, page 31, for the template with directions.)

The protocol in figure 6.10 (page 128) serves as an archive of your team successes, a living plan of next steps, and an honest dialogue about what is currently working or not working for your second-grade students. As you build trust among your team, consider the following guiding questions for supporting transparent and honest dialogue after your common end-of-unit assessment.

- Where in the data do you see a trend to celebrate?

- After looking at your classroom data, what questions would you ask your teammates?

- What would you like to know more about to support one another's mathematical teaching practices?

- Where in the data do you see evidence or need for adjusting your approach to teaching the unit standards?

Questions such as these encourage open reflection on what your team's data is telling you and help you focus your instructional plan moving forward.

Your second-grade team has now identified the essential learning standards from the state standards in the second-grade multidigit addition and subtraction unit. You have worked together to agree on and

Essential Learning Standard	Notes When Planning: What to Emphasize or Remember for Lessons and Assessments in the Unit	Team Reflections After the Unit
I can quickly add within 20. I can quickly subtract within 20.	Being fluent doesn't only mean to answer quickly and accurately; it also involves thinking flexibly about number (NCTM, 2014b). We need to include time for number talks as lesson openers.	Timed drills seem to stress our students. Fluency is not a matter of memorizing facts, but rather as an outcome of a multiyear process that heavily involves practice and reasoning. We plan to use the rubric with student observations because it gave us higher-quality information about our students' fact fluency needs.
I can represent numbers in more than one way using hundreds, tens, and ones.	When teaching, include representations such as base-ten blocks, drawings, and layered three-digit place-value cards to build connections between three-digit numbers and understanding hundreds, tens, and ones. Three-digit place-value cards can help reveal the expanded form of the number.	Revisit representing large numbers throughout the remainder of the year through routines, independent practice, discussions, and other activities. Make sure students are using different groupings of tens and ones for large numbers to support their understanding of regrouping numbers when subtracting.
I can estimate sums and differences within 100 and explain my thinking. I can add and subtract within 100 and explain my thinking.	Students can use models, charts, invented strategies, and number lines to add and subtract numbers to 100. Consider strategies that build on place value. Be sure to practice estimating. Don't teach the algorithm yet. Students often develop misconceptions and have a difficult time explaining and remembering how to use the algorithm without first understanding regrouping with more concrete models.	We were able to find many ways to transform some pencil-and-paper activities to student center games using dice and base-ten blocks. Students were making connections between their picture models and the expanded algorithm. We had fewer subtraction errors than we did on our fall assessment. We need to use more open number lines to see student thinking.
I can add and subtract to solve word problems and show my thinking.	Students must represent problems to develop an understanding of them and how to solve them. Various representations are needed for deep understanding. These representations must be connected to the problem and to equations. Bar diagrams and similar drawings are good choices for representing the relationships within a problem. Students must explain why an operation is needed to solve a problem. It connects to their representations and making sense of the problem. Joining, combining, and adding to are clearly addition situations. Subtraction situations can be solved with either operation.	One teacher used a graphic organizer that helped students with two-step problems. We found that students who defended their thinking and showed their work did better overall on the assessment. We want to include more problem contexts that have the unknown in various places in our lessons.

Overall Unit Reflections: Things to Remember or Change for Next Year

We struggled with finding a shared agreement for proficiency for representing numbers up to 1,000. After a couple of collaborative sessions, we found a proficiency scale we all agreed on. We can use it in our future unit with addition and subtraction within 1,000.

Figure 6.10: Reflection and notes for grade 2 multidigit addition and subtraction unit.

Unit: Grade 2 Multidigit Addition and Subtraction **Start Date:** February 10 **End Date:** March 7 **Total Number of Days:** 19	
Essential Learning Standards	• I can quickly add within 20. • I can quickly subtract within 20. • I can represent numbers in more than one way using hundreds, tens, and ones. • I can estimate sums and differences within 100 and explain my thinking. • I can add and subtract within 100 and explain my thinking. • I can add and subtract to solve word problems and show my thinking.
Prior Knowledge	**Grade 1:** • Compose and decompose within 10 quickly. • Tell the number of tens and ones in a number. • Use strategies to add and subtract within 20. • Add two-digit by one-digit numbers within 100 using different strategies. • Solve word problems using addition or subtraction within 20 with unknowns in all positions.
Vocabulary and Notations	Add Subtract Sum Difference Equal Equation Place value Digit Estimate Notations: Expanded form, +, −, =
Resources and Activities	• Textbook: Chapter 3, Lesson 3.7; Chapter 6, Lessons 6.1–6.10; and Chapter 7, Lesson 7.2 • District-Adopted Fluency Program • Number Talks • Double Dice Plus One game • Double ten-frame images • Missing addends • Base-ten picture cards mix and match • Base-ten riddles • Ways to make a number • Compatible numbers task • Tiered addition and subtraction • Race to a Flat and Race to Zero • Act-it-out problem solving • Numberless word problems • Visualizing task • Create Your Own Story Problem station • Achieve the Core (https://achievethecore.org): Fluency Resources for Grade-Level Routines • Illustrative Mathematics (www.illustrativemathematics.org) tasks: Bundling and Unbundling, Regrouping, Making 124 • Mathematics at Work (go.SolutionTree.com/MathematicsatWork): Figure 3.11: Grade 2 Make Suggestions Example (Norris & Schuhl, 2016)

Figure 6.11: Grade 2 multidigit addition and subtraction unit planner.   continued →

Tools and Technology	• Counters (bears, two-colored counters, square tiles) • Rekenreks • Linking cubes • Base-ten blocks • Ten frames • Open number line • Calculator • Hundreds chart • Place-value chart • National Library of Virtual Manipulatives: nlvm.usu.edu/en/nav/vlibrary.html • Math Playground: www.mathplayground.com/GrandSlammath1.html • Arcademics: www.arcademics.com/games/alien • Greg Tang Math, Math Limbo: https://gregtangmath.com/mathlimbo • Team-developed lessons using SMART Board
Reflection and Notes	When planning: • Being fluent doesn't only mean to answer quickly and accurately, but also involves thinking flexibly about number (NCTM, 2014b). • We are going to make sure to include time for number talks as lesson openers. • When teaching, include representations such as base-ten blocks, drawings, and layered three-digit place-value cards to build connections between three-digit numbers and understanding hundreds, tens, and ones. • Three-digit place-value cards can help reveal the expanded form of the number • Students can use models, charts, invented strategies, and number lines to add and subtract numbers to 100. Consider strategies that build on place value. Be sure to practice estimating. • Don't teach the algorithm yet. Students often develop misconceptions and have a difficult time explaining and remembering how to use the algorithm without first understanding regrouping with more concrete models. • Students must represent problems to develop an understanding of them and how to solve them. Various representations are needed for deep understanding. These representations must be connected to the problem and to equations. Bar diagrams and similar drawings are good choices for representing the relationships within a problem. • Students must explain why an operation is needed to solve a problem. It connects to their representations and making sense of the problem. Joining, combining, and adding to are clearly addition situations. Subtraction situations can be solved with either operation. After the unit: • Timed drills seem to stress our students. Fluency is not a matter of memorizing facts, but rather as an outcome of a multiyear process that involves practice and reasoning. We plan to use the rubric with student observations because it gave us higher-quality information about our students' fact fluency needs. • Revisit representing large numbers throughout the remainder of the year through routines, independent practice, discussions, and other activities. Make sure students are using different groupings of tens and ones for large numbers. • We were able to find many ways to transform some pencil-and-paper activities to student center games using dice and base-ten blocks. • Students were making connections between their picture models and the expanded algorithm. We had fewer subtraction errors than we did on our fall assessment. • We need to use more open number lines to see student thinking. • One teacher used a graphic organizer that helped students with two-step problems. • We found that students who defended their thinking and showed their work did better overall on the assessment. • We want to include more problem contexts that have the unknown in various places in our lessons. Changes for next year: • We struggled with finding a shared agreement for proficiency for representing numbers up to 1,000. After a couple of collaborative sessions, we found a proficiency scale we all agreed on. We can use it in our future unit with addition and subtraction within 1,000.

clarify the prior knowledge, vocabulary and notations, resources and activities, and tools and technology. Along the way and after the unit ended, you recorded reflection and notes. Your team has now successfully generated the information needed to complete the Mathematics Unit Planner for your multidigit addition and subtraction unit.

Grade 2 Multidigit Addition and Subtraction Unit Planner

Your team discussions as you planned the multidigit addition and subtraction unit strengthen your daily lesson design and common assessments. Figure 6.11 (page 129) shows the completed Mathematics Unit Planner for the second-grade multidigit addition and subtraction unit, summarizing your team discussions as shared in this chapter. (See figure 1.2, page 11, for the template with directions.)

The multidigit addition and subtraction unit planner in figure 6.11 (page 129), with its accompanying calendar showing daily learning targets and common assessments (see figure 6.5, page 118), scores high on the Mathematics Unit Planning Rubric in figure 2.2 (page 17). How will your team continue planning

units for the year and document your discussions so your team can learn from them from one unit to the next and one year to the next? How does each of your team mathematics unit plans score against the rubric in figure 2.2 (page 17)? Your challenge as a team is to continue planning for each unit to strengthen both student and teacher learning.

Conclusion

This chapter ends the examples, in chapters 3–6, that together show a learning arc of unit planning by preK, kindergarten, first-, and second-grade teams related to foundations of addition and subtraction.

Although this chapter discusses only one possible exemplar of a second-grade unit for mathematics, each mathematics unit your team builds creates a foundational building block for your team to effectively ensure the learning of students across your grade-level team. Together your team's clarity will maximize your instructional minutes and strengthen your practices. Every member of your team and, more important, every student will benefit as you strive to achieve the self-efficacy promise that each and every student can learn the mathematics standards for second grade.

Mathematics Team Organization

Collaborative teams in a PLC emphasize how they *think* about planning a unit of instruction. . . . In one sense, collaborative unit planning is a perfect example of the simultaneous loose-tight framework in action. The team collaboratively agrees on a number of things that it will be tight about regarding each unit, but will be loose regarding teacher methodology or instructional approaches.

—*Robert Eaker and Janel Keating*

As your team makes sense of the required student learning for every unit, record your shared understanding in the Mathematics Unit Planner in figure 1.2 (page 11). Then, as your team creates artifacts related to answering the four critical questions of a PLC for each unit, determine how to organize your work on a unit-by-unit basis so the team can grow and learn from its work in future years.

How will your team record and store your unit plans, common assessments, data analysis and intervention and extension plans, lesson designs, common independent practice assignments, grading agreements, norms, SMART goals, and other team documents? Figure E.1 shares one possible way to organize folders on a server or drive.

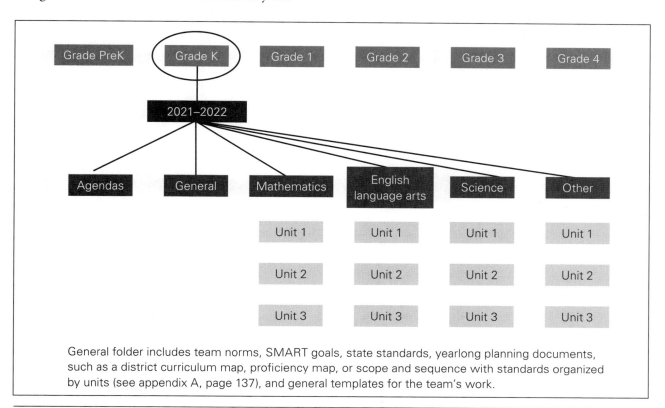

General folder includes team norms, SMART goals, state standards, yearlong planning documents, such as a district curriculum map, proficiency map, or scope and sequence with standards organized by units (see appendix A, page 137), and general templates for the team's work.

Figure E.1: Mathematics team electronic folder organization example.

Rather than storing mathematics team artifacts in topic folders such as *Mathematics Unit Planners, Unwrapped Standards, Common Assessments*, and *Independent Practice*, consider putting each set of team artifacts into its own unit folder. That way, from one year to the next, your team can open *one* folder (the unit folder) to grow your work related to student learning using previously created artifacts.

Once the year ends, copy the current year folder and create a new one with the next school year as its label (along with the name of the unit). Now your team can modify artifacts and continue to deepen your understanding of standards and student learning. Archiving from one year to the next may or may not be necessary. However, sometimes when a team changes an assessment, for example, members realize the previous version was more effective than the newer version; so, the team may want to revert to that previous version in the future. Making sure that document is still available (without recreating it) will save your team some time.

Final Thoughts

While the Mathematics Unit Planner in figure 1.2 (page 11) is critical for your team's shared understanding of the first critical question (What do we expect students to know and be able to do?), it does not produce robust team answers to all four critical PLC at Work questions. Instead, the planner is a framework to use when *doing* the mathematics team and coaching actions required to answer all four critical PLC at Work questions (see figure E.2) as shared in the *Every Student Can Learn Mathematics* series (Kanold et al., 2018).

With mathematics unit plans, your team is well on its way to improving student learning. Congratulations!

Every Student Can Learn Mathematics series' **Team and Coaching Actions Serving the Four Critical Questions of a PLC at Work**	1. What do we want all students to know and be able to do?	2. How will we know if students learn it?	3. How will we respond when some students do not learn?	4. How will we extend the learning for students who are already proficient?
Mathematics Assessment and Intervention in a PLC at Work				
Team action 1: Develop high-quality common assessments for the agreed-on essential learning standards.	▪	▪		
Team action 2: Use common assessments for formative student learning and intervention.			▪	▪
Mathematics Instruction and Tasks in a PLC at Work				
Team action 3: Develop high-quality mathematics lessons for daily instruction.	▪	▪		
Team action 4: Use effective lesson designs to provide formative feedback and encourage student perseverance.			▪	▪
Mathematics Homework and Grading in a PLC at Work				
Team action 5: Develop and use high-quality common independent practice assignments for formative student learning.	▪	▪		
Team action 6: Develop and use high-quality common grading components and formative grading routines.			▪	▪
Mathematics Coaching and Collaboration in a PLC at Work				
Coaching action 1: Develop PLC structures for effective teacher team engagement, transparency, and action.	▪	▪		
Coaching action 2: Use common assessments and lesson-design elements for teacher team reflection, data analysis, and subsequent action.			▪	▪

Source: Kanold, Schuhl, et al., 2018, p. 3.

Figure E.2: Mathematics in a PLC at Work framework from the *Every Student Can Learn Mathematics* series.

*Visit **go.SolutionTree.com/MathematicsatWork** for a free reproducible version of this figure.*

Create a Proficiency Map

If your collaborative team does not have a year-long plan with standards placed in reasonable mathematics units of study, consider organizing your standards using the protocol example for second grade in figure A.1. The resulting document in figure A.2 (page 138) is a proficiency map your team will use to determine when students should be proficient with each standard.

Directions: Determine in which unit students will learn the standards using the following steps.

1. Read each state standard for your grade level or course, and identify when in the school year (in at most a four-week window), or in which chapter of your curriculum materials, students will be proficient with each standard. Write the time frame beside each standard.

2. Group standards together by time of year (or by chapter) to create a scope and sequence of learning. For any standard the team has not yet identified, determine in which grouping it makes sense for students to be proficient with it.

3. Make a table showing the unit names, length of time for each unit, and the standards students will learn in each unit. Use this to create more detailed unit plans and to backward plan the amount of time your team can spend teaching standards in each unit.

Figure A.2 (page 138) shows an example of an unfinished proficiency map. To complete the map, add each standard the team expects students to be proficient with.

State Standard	Unit or Time
2.9. Understand each digit in a three-digit number represents amounts of hundreds, tens, and ones in the number.	Unit 5
2.10. Count within 1,000 starting and ending with any given number.	Unit 5
2.11. Skip count within 1,000 by 5s, 10s, and 100s.	Unit 5
2.12. Read and write numbers to 1,000 using numerals, number names, and expanded form.	Unit 5
2.13. Compare two three-digit numbers using place-value understanding, and record the comparisons using the symbols <, >, or =.	Unit 5
(Continue list with remaining state standards.)	

Figure A.1: Team protocol to organize mathematics standards.

*Visit **go.SolutionTree.com/MathematicsatWork** for a free reproducible version of this figure.*

	Unit 1 (Name) (# Days) Ends:	Unit 2 (Name) (# Days) Ends:	Unit 3 (Name) (# Days) Ends:	Unit 4 (Name) (# Days) Ends:	Unit 5 Three-Digit Place Value 24 Days Ends: Feb 12	Unit 6 (Name) (# Days) Ends:	Unit 7 (Name) (# Days) Ends:	Unit 8 (Name) (# Days) Ends:
Counting and Cardinality								
Operations and Algebraic Thinking								
Number and Operations in Base Ten					2.9 Three-digit number place value 2.10 Count within 1,000 2.11 Skip count by 5s, 10s, and 100s 2.12 Read and write to 1,000 2.13 Compare numbers			
Measurement and Data								
Geometry								

Figure A.2: Team protocol to determine grade-level or course mathematics units.

*Visit **go.SolutionTree.com/MathematicsatWork** for a free reproducible version of this figure.*

Once complete, use the proficiency map to check your team's pacing with learning over the course of the year. If your team decides to extend a unit, will there still be time to teach the essential learning standards in the last unit? If not, which units will the team shorten, or which standards will it omit as nice-to-know standards?

Your team will also use the proficiency map as the outline for the mathematics unit planning this book describes.

Team Checklist and Questions for Mathematics Unit Planning

Your team can use the following checklists to summarize what members should do to complete each part of the Mathematics Unit Planner in figure 1.2 (page 11). (See also the Mathematics Unit Planner and calendar in the *Mathematics at Work Plan Book* [Kanold & Schuhl, 2020, p. 30].)

❶ Generate Essential Learning Standards

❑ Unwrap state standards into daily learning targets by determining what students must know and be able to do.

❑ Rewrite standards in student-friendly language to generate essential learning standards for assessment and reflection.

❑ Identify which state standards in the unit are need-to-know or important-to-know standards.

❑ Create three to six essential learning standards for a unit.

❑ Determine what students must know and be able to do to be proficient with each standard.

❑ Use essential learning standards as the driver for feedback on common assessments, classwork, independent practice, and intervention as a collaborative team.

❑ List essential learning standards in the Mathematics Unit Planner for teachers and students to reference.

❷ Create a Unit Calendar

❑ Determine the start and end dates for the unit.

❑ Determine the dates to administer any common mid-unit and end-of-unit assessments.

❑ Determine each date your team will analyze data from any common mid-unit and end-of-unit assessments to plan a team response to student learning.

❑ Determine when students will learn the essential learning standards. Identify the daily learning targets to address each day (teachers plan their own lessons for the targets, which align to the essential learning standards), so your team collectively determines how to grow student learning throughout the unit.

❑ Consider any holidays, in-service days, field trips, assemblies, or other events that might impact the unit, and, as a team, clarify and emphasize what is most critical for students to learn in the unit.

❑ Consider building in a flex day for your team to use as a response to student learning after a common mid-unit assessment.

❸ Identify Prior Knowledge

❑ Determine the recent prerequisite standards students have learned that they need to access the grade- or course-level content in the current unit.

❑ Summarize each prior-knowledge standard, and add it to the Mathematics Unit Planner.

❑ Determine mathematical tasks students will use to access their prior knowledge at the start of lessons and then throughout the unit. Use these tasks on a short preassessment to determine whether students have learned the skills and to provide feedback to your team and students.

❹ Determine Vocabulary and Notations

❑ Identify the academic vocabulary students will be reading and using in discourse and their work throughout the unit. Include the vocabulary in the Mathematics Unit Planner.

❑ Identify any mathematical notations students will need to read, write, speak, and use during the unit. Include the mathematical notations in the Mathematics Unit Planner.

❑ Determine how students will make sense of and practice using the academic vocabulary and notations throughout the unit.

❺ Identify Resources and Activities

❑ Determine which lessons in the team's current curriculum materials align to the essential learning standards in the unit.

❑ Determine examples of higher- and lower-level tasks students must engage in to fully learn each essential learning standard.

❑ Identify any meaningful explorations, activities, or projects to use across the team to help students learn the essential learning standards.

❑ Determine any supplemental materials students need to fully learn the essential learning standards.

❑ Identify mathematics tasks the team will use in the Mathematics Unit Planner.

❻ Agree on Tools and Technology

❑ Determine any manipulatives or technology students need to learn the essential learning standards.

❑ Identify whether the tools and technology in the unit will support student learning of the essential learning standards with a focus on conceptual understanding, application, or procedural fluency.

❑ Identify which tools and technology, if any, will be part of instruction or available for common assessments.

❼ Record Reflection and Notes

❑ When planning the unit, record notes of things to remember when teaching by considering questions such as, When should students use manipulatives? How will students write their thinking and use notations? What are the expectations for student work when they draw a graph on a coordinate plane? Which strategies should we use?

❑ After the unit, reflect on the unit instruction and assessments your team would like to keep or change next year. Record ideas to use when planning the unit next year.

When completing these checklists for each mathematics unit, your team may want to also answer the following questions to generate quality team discussions related to the mathematics unit plan and its use for further team planning.

❶ Team Questions to Generate Essential Learning Standards

- Which standards in the unit are need-to-know standards and important-to-know standards? Why?

- What are the three to six essential learning standards (the team rewrites in student-friendly *I can* language) for this unit?

- What do the state standards say a student must know and be able to do to be proficient with each essential learning standard?

- When will students learn each essential learning standard during the unit?

- How will your team share the essential learning standards with students at the start of the unit, during the unit, and as feedback after common assessments?

- What are examples of tasks that clarify each essential learning standard?

❷ Team Questions to Create a Unit Calendar

- When does the unit start and end?

- When will you give any common mid-unit assessments? Common end-of-unit assessment?

- When will your team analyze data from each common assessment?

- What is the story arc of learning using daily targets from essential learning standards?

- What dates, if any, will be flex days for student re-engagement?

- Which dates, if any, are holidays, professional development days, or days not allocated for instruction?

❸ Team Questions to Identify Prior Knowledge

- What have students previously learned (this year or during a prior year) that they need to learn each essential learning standard in this unit?

- How will your team access students' prior knowledge during the unit?

- What are examples of tasks or activities to use to activate students' prior knowledge needed for lessons in this unit?

- What is your team plan to address the needs of students who have not yet learned the prior knowledge they need to learn the essential learning standards in this unit (without removing students from learning grade-level standards)?

❹ Team Questions to Determine Vocabulary and Notations

- What are the academic mathematics vocabulary words students must read, speak, and use during this unit to be proficient with the essential learning standards?

- Which mathematical notations will students need to be able to read, write, speak, and use during this unit to be proficient with the essential learning standards?

- How will students learn and repeatedly practice reading, writing, speaking, and listening to the mathematical vocabulary and notations in the unit?

❺ Team Questions to Identify Resources and Activities

- Which lessons in your textbook can your team use to teach the essential learning standards?

- Which tasks in your textbooks can be used to teach the essential learning standards?

- What supplemental materials, if any, does your team need? Where can you access them?

- What are examples of higher- and lower-level tasks students need to be able to do?

- What activities or explorations can your team use to help students develop conceptual understanding of the essential learning standards?

❻ Team Questions to Agree on Tools and Technology

- Which tools or manipulatives do students need to develop conceptual understanding of the essential learning standards?

- How will your team scaffold use of tools or manipulatives (if needed) for students to solve tasks using tools, drawing pictures, and writing equations?

- What technology (hardware) does your team need to advance student learning of essential learning standards?

- Which programs (software) or sites does your team need to advance student learning of essential learning standards?

❼ Team Questions to Record Reflection and Notes

- As your team plans the unit, what do you want all members to remember and record so individual teachers can reference the plan while teaching the unit?

- Which mathematical strategies will your team agree to use to help students learn?

- After the unit, what did your team decide worked well and want to replicate next year?

- After the unit, what did your team decide needs to be revised or changed next year to better grow student learning?

- What will your team need to emphasize next year to close holes in student learning of the essential learning standards?

References and Resources

Achieve the Core. (n.d.). *Coherence map.* Accessed at https://achievethecore.org/coherence-map on January 20, 2020.

Ainsworth, L. (2003). *"Unwrapping" the standards: A simple process to make standards manageable.* Englewood, CO: Advanced Learning Press.

Ainsworth, L. (2004). *Power standards: Identifying the standards that matter the most.* Englewood, CO: Advanced Learning Press.

Bailey, K., & Jakicic, C. (2017). *Simplifying common assessment: A guide for Professional Learning Communities at Work.* Bloomington, IN: Solution Tree Press.

Ben-Hur, M. (2006). *Concept-rich mathematics instruction: Building a strong foundation for reasoning and problem solving.* Alexandria, VA: Association for Supervision and Curriculum Development.

Boaler, J. (2016). *Mathematical mindsets: Unleashing students' potential through creative math, inspiring messages, and innovative teaching.* San Francisco: Jossey-Bass.

Buffum, A., Mattos, M., & Malone, J. (2018). *Taking action: A handbook for RTI at Work.* Bloomington, IN: Solution Tree Press.

Celano, D. C., & Neuman, S. B. (2019). Message in a backpack™: Fun ways to build your child's literacy skills while doing laundry together. *Teaching Young Children, 13*(1). Accessed at www.naeyc.org/resources/pubs/tyc/oct2019/backpack
/build-literacy-doing-laundry on June 5, 2020.

Civil, M., & Turner, E. (2014). Introduction. In M. Civil & E. Turner (Eds.), *Common Core State Standards in mathematics for English language learners: Grades K–8* (pp. 1–5). Alexandria, VA: TESOL Press.

Common Core Standards Writing Team (n.d.). *Progressions documents for the Common Core math standards.* Accessed at https://math.arizona.edu/~ime/progressions/#committee on September 23, 2019.

Conzemius, A. E., & O'Neill, J. (2014). *The handbook for SMART school teams: Revitalizing best practices for collaboration* (2nd ed.). Bloomington, IN: Solution Tree Press.

Cross, C. T., Woods, T. A., & Schweingruber, H. (Eds.). (2009). *Mathematics learning in early childhood: Paths toward excellence and equity.* Washington, DC: National Academies Press.

Dimich, N. (2015). *Design in five: Essential phases to create engaging assessment practice.* Bloomington, IN: Solution Tree Press.

DuFour, R. (2015). *In praise of American educators: And how they can become even better.* Bloomington, IN: Solution Tree Press.

DuFour, R., DuFour, R., Eaker, R., Many, T. W., & Mattos, M. (2016). *Learning by doing: A handbook for Professional Learning Communities at Work* (3rd ed.). Bloomington, IN: Solution Tree Press.

Eaker, R., & Keating, J. (2015). *Kid by kid, skill by skill: Teaching in a Professional Learning Community at Work.* Bloomington, IN: Solution Tree Press.

Fletcher, G. (n.d.). 3-Act tasks: Sheet 1. *GFletchy.* Accessed at https://gfletchy.com/3-act-lessons on September 23, 2019.

Illustrative Mathematics. (n.d.). *Home.* Accessed at www.illustrativemathematics.org on January 20, 2019.

Kanold, T. D., Barnes, B., Larson, M. R., Kanold-McIntyre, J., Schuhl, S., & Toncheff, M. (2018). *Mathematics homework and grading in a PLC at Work.* Bloomington, IN: Solution Tree Press.

Kanold, T. D., Kanold-McIntyre, J., Larson, M. R., Barnes, B., Schuhl, S., & Toncheff, M. (2018). *Mathematics instruction and tasks in a PLC at Work.* Bloomington, IN: Solution Tree Press.

Kanold, T. D., & Schuhl, S. (2020). *Mathematics at Work plan book.* Bloomington, IN: Solution Tree Press.

Kanold, T. D., Schuhl, S., Larson, M. R., Barnes, B., Kanold-McIntyre, J., & Toncheff, M. (2018). *Mathematics assessment and intervention in a PLC at Work.* Bloomington, IN: Solution Tree Press.

Kanold, T. D. (Ed.), Larson, M. R., Fennell, F., Adams, T. L., Dixon, J. K., Kobett, B. M., & Wray, J. A. (2012). *Common Core mathematics in a PLC at Work, grades K–2.* Bloomington, IN: Solution Tree Press.

Kanold, T. D., Toncheff, M., Larson, M. R., Barnes, B., Kanold-McIntyre, J., & Schuhl, S. (2018). *Mathematics coaching and collaboration in a PLC at Work.* Bloomington, IN: Solution Tree Press.

Kilpatrick, J., Swafford, J., & Findell, B. (Eds.). (2001). *Adding it up: Helping children learn mathematics.* Washington, DC: National Academies Press.

Kramer, S. V., & Schuhl, S. (2017). *School improvement for all: A how-to guide for doing the right work.* Bloomington, IN: Solution Tree Press.

Lesh, R., Post, T., & Behr, M. (1987). Representations and translations among representations in mathematics learning and problem solving. In C. Janvier (Ed.), *Problems of representation in the teaching and learning of mathematics* (pp. 33–40). Hillsdale, NJ: Erlbaum.

Many, T. W. (2016, Summer). Is it R.E.A.L. or not? *AllThingsPLC Magazine,* 34–35.

Marzano, R. J. (2003). *What works in schools: Translating research into action.* Alexandria, VA: Association for Supervision and Curriculum Development.

Marzano, R. J. (2004). *Building background knowledge for academic achievement: Research on what works in schools.* Alexandria, VA: Association for Supervision and Curriculum Development.

Marzano, R. J., Warrick, P. B., Rains, C. L., & DuFour, R. (2018). *Leading a high reliability school.* Bloomington, IN: Solution Tree Press.

National Council of Teachers of Mathematics. (2006). *Curriculum focal points for prekindergarten through grade 8 mathematics: A quest for coherence.* Reston, VA: Author.

National Council of Teachers of Mathematics. (2014a). *Principles to actions: Ensuring mathematical success for all.* Reston, VA: Author.

National Council of Teachers of Mathematics. (2014b). *Procedural fluency in mathematics: A position of the National Council of Teachers of Mathematics.* Accessed at www.nctm.org/Standards-and-Positions/Position-Statements /Procedural-Fluency-in-Mathematics/ on May 17, 2020.

National Council of Teachers of Mathematics. (2018). *Catalyzing change in high school mathematics: Initiating critical conversations.* Reston, VA: Author.

National Council of Teachers of Mathematics. (2020). *Catalyzing change in early childhood and elementary mathematics: Initiating critical conversations.* Reston, VA: Author.

National Governors Association Center for Best Practices & Council of Chief State School Officers. (2010). *Common Core State Standards for mathematics.* Washington, DC: Authors. Accessed at www.corestandards.org/assets/CCSSI _Math%20Standards.pdf on January 20, 2020.

National Mathematics Advisory Panel. (2008). *Foundations for success: The final report of the National Mathematics Advisory Panel.* Washington, DC: U.S. Department of Education.

Neugebauer, S. R., Hopkins, M., & Spillane, J. P. (2019). Social sources of teacher self-efficacy: The potential of teacher interactions and proximity to instruction. *Teachers College Record, 121*(4), 13–21.

Norris, K., & Schuhl, S. (2016). *Engage in the mathematical practices: Strategies to build numeracy and literacy with K–5 learners*. Bloomington, IN: Solution Tree Press.

Reeves, D. B. (2002). *The leader's guide to standards: A blueprint for educational equity and excellence*. San Francisco: Jossey-Bass.

Smith, M. S., & Stein, M. K. (1998). Selecting and creating mathematical tasks: From research to practice. *Mathematics Teaching in the Middle School, 3*(5), 344–350.

Utah State University. (n.d.). *National Library of Virtual Manipulatives*. Accessed at http://nlvm.usu.edu/en/nav/vlibrary .html on September 23, 2019.

Wiggins, G., & McTighe, J. (1998). *Understanding by design*. Alexandria, VA: Association for Supervision and Curriculum Development.

Wiggins, G., & McTighe, J. (2011). *The understanding by design guide to creating high-quality units*. Alexandria, VA: Association for Supervision and Curriculum Development.

Wilkins, J. L. M. (1997). *Modeling correlates of problem-solving skills: Effects of opportunity to learn on the attainment of higher-order thinking skills in mathematics*. Unpublished doctoral dissertation, University of Illinois at Urbana-Champaign, IL.

Index

Every Student Can Learn Mathematics series
Timothy D. Kanold et al.
Discover a comprehensive PLC at Work® approach to achieving mathematics success in K–12 classrooms. Each book offers two teacher team or coaching actions that empower teams to reflect on and refine current practices and routines based on high-quality, research-affirmed criteria.
BKF823 BKF824 BKF825 BKF826

Mathematics Assessment and Intervention in a PLC at Work®
Timothy D. Kanold, Sarah Schuhl, Matthew R. Larson, Bill Barnes, Jessica Kanold-McIntyre, and Mona Toncheff
Harness the power of assessment to inspire mathematics learning. This user-friendly resource shows how to develop high-quality common assessments, and effectively use the assessments for formative learning and intervention. The book features unit samples for learning standards, sample unit exams, and more.
BKF823

Mathematics Homework and Grading in a PLC at Work®
Timothy D. Kanold, Bill Barnes, Matthew R. Larson, Jessica Kanold-McIntyre, Sarah Schuhl, and Mona Toncheff
Rely on this user-friendly resource to help you create common independent practice assignments and equitable grading practices that boost student achievement in mathematics. The book features teacher team tools and activities to inspire student achievement and perseverance.
BKF825

Mathematics Coaching and Collaboration in a PLC at Work®
Timothy D. Kanold, Mona Toncheff, Matthew R. Larson, Bill Barnes, Jessica Kanold-McIntyre, and Sarah Schuhl
Build a mathematics teaching community that promotes learning for K–12 educators and students. This user-friendly resource will help you coach highly effective teams within your PLC and then show you how to utilize collaboration and lesson-design elements for team reflection, data analysis, and action.
BKF826

Solution Tree | Press *a division of*
Solution Tree

Visit SolutionTree.com or call 800.733.6786 to order.

GL⬤BAL PD

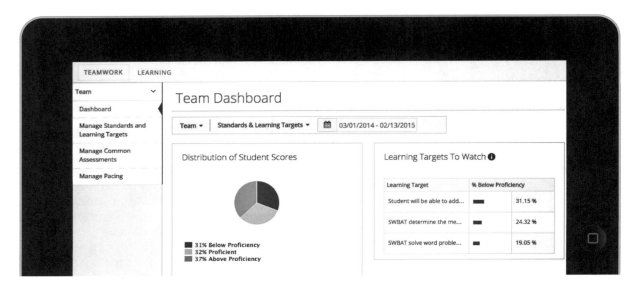

The **Power to Improve**
Is in Your Hands

Global PD gives educators focused and goals-oriented training from top experts. You can rely on this innovative online tool to improve instruction in every classroom.

- Get unlimited, on-demand access to guided video and book content from top Solution Tree authors.

- Improve practices with personalized virtual coaching from PLC-certified trainers.

- Customize learning based on skill level and time commitments.

Solution Tree

Solution Tree's mission is to advance the work of our authors. By working with the best researchers and educators worldwide, we strive to be the premier provider of innovative publishing, in-demand events, and inspired professional development designed to transform education to ensure that all students learn.

The National Council of Teachers of Mathematics advocates for high-quality mathematics teaching and learning for each and every student.